D1558992

MISS SUE AND THE SHERIFF

Miss Sue
and the Sheriff

By ROBERT BURTON HOUSE

CHAPEL HILL

The University of North Carolina Press

1941

B

House

Copyright, 1941, by

The University of North Carolina Press

Printed in the United States of America by

Van Rees Press, New York

01257994

Preface

THESE SKETCHES began with "Miss Sue and the Sheriff," which I wrote as a memorial to my father and mother. My family and friends urged me to add to them, and I have done so.

I wish to express appreciation to the Raleigh, N. C., *News and Observer* for printing the sketches, which appeared as "The Biography of a Southern Home" in the Sunday editions from January 14 to March 24, 1940. And my thanks go especially to Louis Graves, of Chapel Hill, who made suggestions helping me with the first number, and to Frank Smethurst of the *News and Observer* who helped me with suggestions about the whole series.

R. B. House

Chapel Hill, N. C.
June, 1941

Contents

MISS SUE AND THE SHERIFF

Miss Sue and the Sheriff

WELL, ANYWAY, I kept you from marrying Willie Dillahay," said my father. Whereupon Uncle Charlie snickered and gave a ribald imitation of a drunk man singing "Oh, can't you hear me, Susie, darling," then laughed and said, "He was three miles away." Mamma blushed, laughed; and the incident passed off. All it was, anyway, was a family joke as to whether Papa was really good enough for her. I am quite sure that for all his joking Papa knew in his heart, as he showed in his manner, that she was a gracious gift of God and that nobody was good enough for her. He would mount his high horse and parade before anybody else, but not before her quiet smile. She was his poetry, his romance, his symbol of fineness, as well as his wife and companion. It might be all controversy between us and him unless the point pressed into this finer realm. If it did, he passed one verdict and obeyed

the decision: "Ask your Mammy." He was deeply and
sometimes violently emotional and never got over being
ashamed of his emotions. No man ever loved his children more than he did or was more dumb in asking
and showing affection. "Write to your Mammy," he
would say as we went on our several journeys. That
meant he would get the letter, too, sometimes to read
if the chirography did not bore him, but most fre-
quently to enjoy through her. "What does Rob say?"
he would ask, and listen to her account and comment.
He knew that every detail was engraved on her heart,
and that heart was his breviary.

I grew up in a sincere conviction that Miss Sue and
General Lee were the finest achievements of the South.
And, as to Papa, I put him in the same class, on the
ground that he could appreciate them and give them
his complete loyalty. He would have charged any
breastwork that General Lee ordered him to; but he
would have done it solely to protect Miss Sue and her
flock and to bring back to her whatever might lie
behind it. He demonstrated, though only five years old
when the war ended its military phase, the complete
qualities of a soldier of the Confederacy. He knew what
the historians do not yet know so well as he did, that the
war never really ended, since it was a clash of ideals. And

he had his ideal ever before him. He was married to it. He was a farmer, a mechanic, a county politician in his working. He was a knight-errant in his heart, having achieved the miracle of his lady without losing his romance. He played Sancho Panza to his own Don Quixote, for his upbringing was tough in those hard-bitten years—broad, salty, vulgar, sweaty, catch-as-catch-can. But the ideal was in him, and the artist touch of Miss Sue brought it out.

He gave her the name, "Miss Sue," when she came into the neighborhood as a school teacher, became his Sunday school teacher, and won his heart. It was stubborn material for her to work with, not gentled yet or tamed. But Willie Dillahay, who felt her spell for a time, slumped back. The heart of Papa responded to the call. She had back of her the agrarian tradition of Six-Pound in Warren County, as nearly the Virginia tradition as is found in North Carolina, as near the tradition of true gentleman and true lady as is found anywhere.

Travis helped to fix the name. Travis had been a slave in my mother's home, and had run away to Halifax County, finding a home with my father's family at Edgewood. It was Travis who came to take the horse when Papa drove up with Miss Sue as his bride. His black face became illuminated with that smile of complete, humorous, spiritual understanding which played over it every time he saw Miss Sue. Negro gossip and rumor would have it at times that "they" were going to put the Negroes back into slavery. "It don't make no difference to me if they do," Travis would snicker. "Ise already with my mistis."

The neighbors took up the name and confirmed it. Even we children used it in referring to her, though she was "Mamma" when we spoke to her, a part of "Papa'n'Mamma" which was the vital harmony of our life. "Miss Sue" was the title of the queen, the source of final authority which operated solely through the power of love and understanding.

"The finest thing about the schools," my mother often remarked, "was simply that they brought fine girls into neighborhoods, and that the children caught from them the little touches of fine character, fine attitudes, and fine manners." She was thinking of girls other than herself, for her regard was ever on others. But her hearers nodded approval because they had before them the illustration of what she was talking about. "Ain't this Miss Sue's little Rob?" some black or white neighbor would say, fixing in the mind of the child a sense of *noblesse oblige*. A nation could leave its destiny safely under such influences as her teaching and mothering.

She had left the broad sweep of farm acres and the gentle cleanness of the farmstead for a home dominated by machinery—sawmills, gristmills, machine shops; there was even machinery in the house itself. The Sheriff was a collector of the biggest junk pile in the county—junk to others, but to him broken possibilities of salvaging and mechanical redemption. Miss Sue had taken her stand long before the Nashville agrarians; she inherited it whole and operative. Generations in English Devonshire, in Virginia, and in North Carolina, had confirmed it. Land, fields, woods, the procession of the seasons, the poetry of L'Allegro were in it. Machinery was in Josie's world (Josie was her name for my father) and to be handled loyally as was any other inexplicable fact in Josie's world. But it was not in her world. Hence, she hung up pictures of cows and landscapes with the tools and pieces of engines, and contemplated the pictures with her soul. She would have preferred candles to the lamp, but she infinitely preferred the lamp to the electric bulb. And, though she submitted to Josie's putting in the electric bulb, she was sure that some day the thing would explode in her face.

Josie loved gasoline, not only for its brisk efficiency in stepping along in the form of engines, but as a substitute for soap, as a disinfectant and germicide. There was always a smell of gasoline about his manipulations with things. In her fixed opinion he was playing momently with death. A mowing machine, an engine, a sawmill, she viewed with amazement. The only ride she ever enjoyed in an automobile was when it broke down and was towed in by a pair of mules. She did not retreat from the world of machinery; she simply remained on her own known and loved agrarian premises.

Machinery, money, politics, were to her facts in the world of men. This world she respected and served. It was the world of the provider. Her business was that of consumer and dispenser of provisions brought in by Josie. What he did was too wonderful for her to understand. She was naïvely grateful, and dependent on him for the substance of living. She was sure and artistic only in transmitting this substance into living by the womanly arts. But she would have died in the kitchen before she would have allowed Josie or any other man to get his own breakfast.

There was in her philosophy a definite man's world and a definite woman's world. Men were to be sent out

with confidence and welcomed back with affection—
never to be questioned. If that world was rough, the
only antidote in her philosophy was to woo them out
of roughness by the beauty and peace of home. Josie
went out from Miss Sue and the children to whatever
chore farming, machine work, lumbering, politics,
sheriffing, might entail. He came back to Miss Sue
and the children as to a haven.

She had seen men deteriorate under the shock of
war and reconstruction into loafers and drunkards.
But she still held them to be knights, regarding their
major commitments and not the accidents of the fray.
No man was a bad man in her eyes; he was simply a
good man in confusion. If she had anything to say to
him it was in terms of sympathy, understanding and
healing. "Won't you come into the fire, Mr. Tucker?"
she asked one old veteran. "No'm, I thank ye," he replied. "I'm not cold. I've got on drawers. They're the
warmest things I've ever seen in my life. I never expect
to do without them again as long as I live." There was
the whole homely story of war, privation, and an
emerging standard of comfort, each detail of which
she savored.

Men worked, played, fought, hunted, fished. They
might come in with food to cook or mangled bodies

to nurse. She was ready for either eventuality. On one Thanksgiving morning the yard awoke to clamor with the arrival of a wagon bringing in a man shot through the lungs. There had been a pitched battle in the Roanoke River lowgrounds between two parties of Federal revenue officers. Each party had been independently searching for moonshiners. They ran together in the swamps; each mistook the other for the moonshiners; and a pitched battle ensued. Mr. Chapman from Richmond was the wounded man. He stayed in our home under her ministrations until he was well. Old Gaston, a mile and a quarter away, had twenty-five inhabitants and three saloons. It was a hell-hole of drunkenness and brawling. One night our household was startled by the rattling of the front door and the cry, "Is there a man in the house? Is there a man in the house? Tell him to help me, quick!" Some poor tramp asleep over a fire had been set upon by a thug, beaten and robbed. He had run to the big white house for refuge. He was taken in and succored. The railroad ran by the house, the Depot was not far away. The night train unloaded individuals and families in the darkness. All came as a matter of course to our door for lodging, food, transportation. All of them stayed as guests. Organ grinders with their monkeys, tramps, pack-men, found here a matter-of-course welcome. Railroad men, surveyors, hunting parties from "the North" put up with us as though we had been a hotel, but one that presented no bill. Engineers, conductors, brakemen, levied friendly tribute on apples and watermelons and saluted the house as they passed on the trains. All were heirs apparent to the hospitality of Miss Sue and her establishment.

She was in the tradition of the plantation mistress—a tradition of physical endurance and resourcefulness in meeting any emergency. Twenty-one people sat down at her table every day. There were Papa'n'Mamma and their family of ten; Ung' Charlie 'n' Aa Lula and their family of five. There were Grandma and Aa Winnie, the teacher; besides, some forty hands ate out of the kitchen. Whatever the work—cooking, mending, nursing, churning, she was leader in work and director. I never knew her to make but one request: "Give me time; don't confuse me." And yet, in sickness or in health, no matter how long and crowded the day, I never saw her go to bed without spending an hour or two with her books. She read, not for improvement, but for joy. Theocritus depicts a vase on which there is an image of a man fishing. He says that the man was all fishing. Miss Sue under the lamp was all reading. If I could paint her picture with her books, with it I could teach a nation to read.

She knew those books acknowledged to be great. But she knew the art of independent finding. She appreciated greatness regardless of vogue: C. A. Stephens in the *Youth's Companion, Anne of Avonlea,* Joseph C. Lincoln, *The Farm Journal,* as published by the Wilmer Atkinson Company of Philadelphia. But she was expert in every scrap that was ever published on the old South, the War, Reconstruction. She died before *Gone with the Wind* was written. She would have revelled in that book. She did not write about books. She talked little about them. She loved them. One found oneself reading by the spell of her presence with books. Her culture was such as is caught and not taught.

There was no public school in the neighborhood when her flock was ready for a teacher. She, therefore, selected a teacher and set up a school in the yard at home. It was a place of books and of leisurely individual study. Each student made his program with the teacher and progressed, receded, reviewed, and took in new territory as he grew. There was one standard applicable to all: the difference between good work and shoddy work. It was a stern school, therefore, not hesitating to assail the outworks of the person, if the inward spirit proved recalcitrant. It was an autonomous world. A snivelling tale of a whipping at school simply brought on a whipping at home. It required tough minds and enduring bodies. Its subject matter was staple: mastery of language and mathematics. Its prospects were inviting: go as far as you could, go a little farther by stimulated effort. It had no day of graduation, no problem of placement. Its students swung between work in school and work on farm, in the sawmill, in the shop, until gradually they found school receding and the job of work becoming permanent. But it was also a school of play and hobbies. No day's school tasks robbed the students of long hours of games in the yard or of long hours of private reading and wise fooling around. The work of the school came to test in meeting maturing situations of practical work. One student left after three terms to do a man's work at fifteen. Another left and became a locomotive engineer at fourteen. But the workman renewed himself in the home, and the school was a part of the home. Books, games, music, especially singing around the piano, were elements of the school's artful extension as adult education. It was a spirit. The spirit was that of Miss Sue and her books. In the later day of

public schools she loyally rejoiced in more equal op-
portunities for all children. In fact, the school at home
had been kept open to neighboring children at all
times. But she was adamant on quality and individual
interest. "They come and go a great deal," she said of
the public-school children, "but I don't ever see them
sitting down to read any fine thing."

While Miss Sue drew strength from her traditions
and her books, pictures, and music, she expressed her
strength as mother of her children. Strength it was in
epic proportions. She bore ten children without ever
finding out, as a neighbor expressed it, that having a
baby was a major operation. She enjoyed the occasion
of each baby's arrival as a month's vacation in her room.
Each one of her children was to her a fresh introduc-
tion to the universe, a fresh challenge to her power of
attention. While she remained apart from Josie's world
of machinery, she managed to enter the world of her
machinist sons. One became an engineer on the Seaboard Air Line Railway. Immediately she became an
expert on the personnel and schedule of every train on
that railroad. She knew every engineer and fireman,
every conductor and brakeman. They were now a part
of her world for they were the companions of her son.
It was her delight to prepare meals for them. Her orig-

inal impulse was to feed Arthur. But her hospitality
included everybody in his train crew. Through her
sons she learned the workings of the sawmill and the
machine shop. It was her nature to know them and
every detail of what they were doing. She was deaf,
and travelling gave her a headache. Early in life she
ceased to travel and sat in her corner. She followed
her children with her mind's eye and received them in
her corner by the bookstand and the lamp. Nor in all
her life did they fail to visit her there. She wrote them
letters which were transcripts of home. She read their
letters, both the lines and between the lines. One son
was at Chapel Hill. This meant that no one read
more about Chapel Hill than she, or savored its
entire flavor better. She was the most appreciative
reader of Louis Graves' *Chapel Hill Weekly*. With
a son at Harvard she became in spirit a New Eng-
lander, with only one reservation—a fear that he
might marry one of those "Northern girls." And when
a son went to France in the World War she learned
France. She knew her traditions, she knew her home,
she knew her children. They were, in her opinion,
equal to any occasion anywhere. It was her part to
love them into the fine interpretations of the situation.

Her life was based on God; her prayers and her

Bible were her constant sacrament. But she was no talker about religion. On one occasion she did say enough for me to remember that her favorite text was: "The eternal God is my refuge; and underneath are the everlasting arms"; she lived this and raised her family by it. If there was ever a question in her mind of a religious nature it was when our sister died at the age of twenty. But her agony was expressed to her God, and the "why" grief thinks to ask eternally found its answer in sources too deep for my expression.

She left her childhood home in old Six-Pound in Warren County and came to Edgewood in Halifax, only twenty-five miles away. But twenty-five years passed before she saw Six-Pound again. Her passion for it was a constant force; its image was ever before her. Her mood in regard to it was ever one of deep poetic and historic reminiscence over its dear people and scenes. Her children have etched in their minds pictures of Mamma's days in Six-Pound, as of some fairyland. But to marry and to settle down in her new home, her husband, the care of her children, were commitments of her whole spirit. In happy concentration on each day with them she simply never got around to re-visiting Warren County.

There was in her no conflict of interests as between

Martha and Mary; she combined them in such a person as the Master would have gone back in the kitchen to talk to. At any rate the ministers of the Gospel found her such a person. I never saw her in church a great deal; it was understood by all that deafness made it impracticable for her to go. But her children went by the example of a spirit that ministered to the church, and the church came to her corner by the lamp and the reading table, with the Sheriff opposite her by the fire.

In the autumn afternoon of yesterday I stood and looked up the hill so that the slanting rays of the sun met my eyes across the eaves of the old house—the old house that had its beginning before the Revolution as the oak-log cabin of a settler. The cabin is now the dining room, and fourteen other rooms have grown to it in sprawling fashion. To the left by the railroad the sun caught the lines of the burying ground where Miss Sue sleeps beside the Sheriff. In the flooding light, broken by shadows across the fields—here I seemed to catch the image of her smile.

II

The Burdens of Youth

M
Y FIRST RECOLLECTION is of the quiet voice of my oldest sister, Sallie, reassuring me:

"Yes, you are three years old."

This settled an argument with John and Harry about my age. I had already begun to feel the weight of youth in the pursuit of happiness, and was eager to grow old rapidly without bothering to do it gracefully. The older one got, the more freely one seemed to do what one pleased.

It was consideration of the abilities of John and Harry that moved me. The power and glory and freedom of Papa and Uncle Charlie were quite beyond envy, as was the quieter status of Mamma and Aunt Lula, Grandma, and Aunt Winnie. Nor was I concerned to compare my limits with the large freedom of the older boys and girls. Arthur, the oldest, was so nearly a man that he was ready to embark on his career on the railroad. He was always kind to me and would take me with him to get the mail from Old Gaston, riding Charlie with me perched like a horsefly behind him. Henry was learning to saw at the mill and could also lead a band of reapers through the wheat fields. He could go on trips with the wagon. And with Arthur he would go off at night. The Negroes told me they were "goin' courtin'."

Sallie was already gracious and competent in quieting my fears and worries and in rescuing me from dangers. Fannie was fast becoming so. Ernest, Joe, and Charles could give a good account of themselves in "work," something that I considered as a more skillful form of play. All these seemed to be beyond jealous comparisons.

But John and Harry, only two years older than I, seemed to enjoy all the skills and to look into all the mysteries. They could ride like Indians on all the horses and mules, undaunted even after Old Modoc threw John at the pump and trampled on him. They could milk all the cows, even the wild Ida who had to be tied in a brake. She would kick and rear till she got down on her back, glaring at her milker with indignant eyes. They could run down any chicken in the yard with Rex, the bird dog. They knew where all the turkeys nested. And they were masters of the yearling steers, Buck and Ball. They elicited wonder from the Negroes, and were called "little men" by the white grown-ups. They could go away to thin corn in the low-grounds and stay all day.

With their inseparable companion, the Negro Davy, they would prepare for great expeditions into parts unknown as yet to me. When I would sneak up to go with them, they would spurn me with open contempt. Davy would look noncommittal, and Rex would look bored. I would turn back to console myself with Joe, the second-best dog, but he was consumed with jealousy of Rex, and would respond only with a faint howl of commiseration and rap three times on the ground with his tail, like the speaker of a meeting calling me to order.

Nor would appeals to the grown-folks do me any good. "You are not old enough yet," was the refrain that stimulated me to desire much age. Besides, I wanted to grow large and lick the station agent who tormented me all the time about my thin legs and called me "Bicycle Spokes." And I felt isolated. Charles and Joe were paired, John and Harry were paired, in age-levels above me. Hugh and Helen (the twins) and Sue, were at an age-level below me. Mary and Norman, the babies, were paired. I was in between. I aspired to be classed with John and Harry. I had to accept classification with Hugh, Helen, and Sue, to remain as yet definitely one of the small fry. For the present we had to be taken anywhere that we got to go.

Some of the children had nurses. I had none. A Negro girl had tried me for three days, but had gone crazy on the job. None of us had nurses for long. We simply went with the grown-folks, with the older children when they would let us, but chiefly with the Negro men and women as they worked. Our most regular guardian was Snovy, the mastiff, who watched over us with the dignity and fidelity of a Roman soldier. She would leave her station only long enough to chase a rabbit with inexorable strides, catch it, and swallow it down in two giant gulps.

In the house there was a long succession of cooks and maids of all work. When Aunt Liza was in the kitchen she would not apparently be aware of us, but she watched us. Sarah simply laughed with us and told us yarns; she was an edition in charcoal of Chaucer's Wife of Bath. It was hard to get Nancy to come to work at all, but when she did come she was so delightful with her gossip that we waited on her just to hear her talk. Lou, Becky, Aunt Mimy, would take us to visit them in their houses. We feared and respected Aunt Charlotte, who quarrelled with us about our manners. And we tormented Aunt Sallie Gus, who, as midwife, had washed and dressed us when we were born and given us a piece of fat meat to suck. Her lore of assafetida in little bags around our necks, of mullein syrup and onion syrup, impressed our mothers 'and dominated the other Negro women. The Negroes feared her as a conjure woman and because of her prowess. They told us that when she got mad enough to fight she would wait until night, strip stark naked, and go out to waylay her victim with a club. She was kind to us, but excitable, and she would jabber at us in a strange tongue. She told us she was an Ebo and descended from very black kings and queens in Africa.

As to the men, Travis was supreme in the yard and around the lot. He taught us manners by beaming at us when we were good and looking uncompromisingly stern when we were bad. Bill would tote us on his back anywhere. Frank, Joe, Horace, would let us ride the gentler horses to and from the plow, and look out for us around the sawmill and the gin. Reuben would delight us by singing for us when he whetted his cradle in the wheat, beating out a rhythm with his tarred paddle. Frank would guard us from the belts and teeth of the threshing machine, and let us ride when, gypsy-like, it went on caravans to new threshing stations over the neighborhood. George, the fireman at the mill, would let us blow the whistle when it was time.

Matthy, the blacksmith, allowed us to pump the bellows at the forge. We had to remember not to call Matthy a Negro. He called himself a "Portygese." There were many like him. The Negroes called them "No Nations." The grown white-folks called them "Free Issue." One of them, Ananias, would peck the millstones to sharpen them. But the miller, another Bill, seemed to be a sort of connecting link between the whites and the blacks. He had been a Confederate soldier, and from him I first heard that the war had been "a rich man's war but a poor man's fight."

Uncle Barney lived on the place, but rarely did any work. He made a particular point of paying rent. He would bring in a bag of cotton on his back and joke with "Little Boss," as the Negroes called Uncle Charlie. But he would always be forgiven the rent and carry it back, smoking a big cigar which he had bummed off "Little Boss." Barney was our official loafer, liar, and fortune-teller. He lived by his imagination, making up great stories of "working on the bres' works" during the war and of varmints and hoop snakes he met while he was fishing. But Barney got religion. It struck him, he said, in the muscle of his arm when he was coming home from Sis Julie's prayer meeting. He saw visions of torment, millions of human souls seething around in hell like meal bran in boiling water. He saw visions of redemption in which an angel came down from heaven and showed him a new dollar and told him that his soul was now newly minted like the dollar. The Lord took him in a trance to "the Land of Capok" and gave him a robe, a gold harp, a gold crown, and gold shoes.

"Oh go away, Uncle Barney," said his nephew June. "You know there ain't enough gold in heaven to make you a pair of shoes." But Barney resisted ridicule, held to his vision of a new life, and died in the odor of sanctity.

Another Reuben was the special favorite of Papa and Uncle Charlie. He had gone to school with them and boasted that he had the best education to be had, the Bible and Davie's *University Arithmetic*. By the old gin house there was a walnut tree in the fork of which Uncle Charlie had once thrown Reuben in a wrestling match and hung him by his heels. Reuben also achieved the remarkable feat of running after a sheep, falling into a ditch on his head, and spraining his ankle.

When the Negroes came to Uncle Charlie's room on Saturday night to get their pay, we thought it was simply a social occasion and that they, like us, were merely getting money for fun from the bounty of Papa and Uncle Charlie.

We had the farm animals to win us into friendship with them. All the horses, mules, and cows we knew in their individualities, with black marks against only Modoc, the horse, and Brindle, the cow who had all but thrown Sue into the well.

The lesser animals we petted, but we ate them all in good time without feeling too much like cannibals. We salted the sheep, held them for the shearers, and put tar on their noses. We rejoiced in the lambs on their first appearance, gambolling in February; we rejoiced no less in their final delectable appearance as hash in August. We fed the hogs and scratched them into grunting luxury in their pens until such time as they went under the knife on a cold day in November. Then, after being scalded and scraped at the steam trough under the mill shed, they would lie frozen and white, ready for cutting up at the smokehouse. We would then cut off their tails and roast them in the fire, foretasting in their succulence the richer flavors of smack-bones and sausage. The soft-spoken Negro,

Belle, would prepare the sausage and smack-bones in the house. Some of us, to the outspoken disgust of the others, would look forward to chit'lings. These Nancy prepared in the office, while Aunt Sallie Gus "rendered" the lard, and jabbered in terror lest we fall into the pots of well-nigh incandescent grease and cracklings.

We went with the Negro men through the whole procession of crops, feeling the tickle of the freshly broken ground on our newly-bared feet in spring, thinning corn and chopping cotton in the summer, with many a rest under the plum nursery and with many a loitering trip to the spring. We picked cotton and peas in the fall and romped on the wagons that hauled them to the gin. Travis saw that we did not fall off. We had all the resources of wheat stacks, cotton piles, cottonseed piles, and sawdust piles to tumble in. We had belts, saws, and wheels to turn in the shop with the kindly oversight of elders to caution us, "Scat, you scalawags!," if we got into danger. Only one thing brought a sure whipping: that was to play on the railroad.

Papa would take us sheriffing with him and let us drive the horse. We got acquainted with him that way, and by scratching his head and tickling his feet for him in his room at night. He loved for us to do this as he sat, mused, talked, and smoked "Greenback" in a long-stemmed pipe.

Uncle Charlie would take us with him all over the farm, to the logwoods, and in a canoe to the low-grounds. He took us in swimming, to fish-fries and picnics, and to the Weldon Fair and Norfolk. He organized our games in the yard. He sang funny songs to us as he played the guitar in his room at night. And he amazed us by his ability to spit tobacco juice cleanly across the room through a hole in the fire-screen.

But with all this crowding life, I still longed for a more complete liberty to pursue a more adventurous happiness. I wanted to go with John and Harry.

One day they let me: it was to go fishing, provided I helped them pull up their stint of weeds in the garden. We got away and fished all the way down the Barnfield Branch. We paused to gather wild strawberries in the Long Field.... John jumped back from the ditch bank crying,

"I put my hand on a snake!"

There he was, a moccasin, all coiled, beady-eyed, menacing, not at all the insinuating tempter of the Genesis story. Even the dogs recoiled from his malevolent presence.

We fished up Sledge's Branch, and down the creek,

unmindful of gathering clouds until the lightning flicked the tree-tops and the thunder roared in the hills. We began to run home. That trip was a revelation in distances, mystery, and terror. But we made it.

It was good to hear Grandma's ironic greeting:

"Fisherman's luck!

Wet tail and hungry gut."

It was good even to wash my feet on the back porch, grateful for security that went along with discipline.

It was good to wait at supper with the small-fry, and to go to bed without protest. I was content to bear with a lighter heart the burdens of youth.

III

Not Without Tears

"THIS IS 'C' and that is 'F'," said Aunt Winnie, calling me to her in school. I was playing in the schoolroom, which was in "the Store" in the corner of our yard. The building had really been a store once, but Papa and Uncle Charlie were forced to close it in self-defense. The charge accounts were eating up the mercantile business. Most of the hardware they had used in other businesses. The groceries and drygoods Mamma and Aunt Lula had used up in the house. The candy we children had eaten from jars. These jars, subsequently broken, remained on the shelves; just the sort we hunt so avidly as antiques today. The rats ate up the account books. The front room, which was the store proper, remained locked, still a mystery to us beyond the door leading to it from the back room where Aunt Winnie kept school. Sometimes yet, something needed here or there could be produced from the store's dwindled stock. The rats remained as impudent commentators on our labors; they would go "buggity, buggity" in battalions over our heads each day.

For the Store was a failure as a store, the only failure ever permitted by Papa and Uncle Charlie in their magnificent competence otherwise to do anything in the world of work. For mercantile purposes we had two neighbors, one just across the road. He ran a part-time store, sharing his time between it and a small farm. If we could get a cent occasionally out of our constant pleas to Papa and Uncle Charlie, we could go and bang on a piece of old circular saw to call the farmer-merchant from his fields a mile away. A cent was a lot of money. One could purchase with it a stick of candy six inches long, a sugar cake as large as a dinner plate, a stick of round, long, tallow-like chewing gum, or a piece of cheese about as large as one's three fingers. Our neighbor would walk the mile and wait patiently while we looked over his stock and decided on our purchases. He never violated our sense of dignity in the transaction. Often he gave us more than we paid for.

On this neighboring store porch the black and white neighbors would laugh and talk while we studied in the schoolroom across the road. The sound of their laughter would intrigue us. Occasionally some acquaintance, now advanced in years beyond formal schooling, would insult us from the porch by aping the spelling lesson—"B-a-ba-, k-e-r-ker, baker!"

Our other merchant neighbor kept a store up the hill at the cross-roads a mile away. We admired and loved him for his business acumen and for his meek kindliness. When he was a poor boy a friend had given him ten cents. He spent the ten cents for peanuts, roasted the peanuts, sold them and re-invested his capital and profits. From this small start he had built a large store. His store building showed definite divisions in its structure where he had added to it as he prospered. He was too meek to stand up for his rights, even in his store, and so kind that he made our errands to him a delight.

Across the yard from the schoolroom was the house. We could hear the girls strumming on the piano at their music lessons in the parlor. We could see Mamma and Aunt Lula busy with tasks on the front porch and at the well-house. Close by were the sawmill, the gristmill, the gin, the wood-shop, and the blacksmith shop, all resonant with characteristic sounds. All around were the buildings and the lots and fields of the farm. Edging in were the woods in the distance, making the wood-dominated scene the basis of our place's name,

"Edgewood." Bisecting the whole were the road with passing carts and wagons, and the railroad on which the trains passed, not as remote and impersonal things, but as beings intimately and personally known to us by many inspections of equipment and personnel.

Aunt Winnie, Mamma's sister, who taught the school, though she lived with us nine months each year, had seen each of us born, had washed us, dressed us, petted us, spanked us, laughed over us, and cried over us, was, nevertheless, not our governess. She was a teacher. And school, though primarily supported by Papa and Uncle Charlie, was not simply our own private school. It was used by neighbors from near and far, boys and girls, and even young men and young women. But school joined us all together in an atmosphere of intimacy with the homes and the work of the neighborhood. The public school was not taken seriously yet as a school.

Though I was too young to be a pupil, school fascinated me because all the children except the babies were to be found there. So I was allowed to play at going to school. Books fascinated me because Mamma always had a book. Even when she moved around she carried one, marking the place with her finger. And at the well-house she churned and read by the hour. Books in themselves fascinated me. I loved the sight of them, the feel of them, the smell of them, the sound of them as the pupils read aloud.

The little game begun by Aunt Winnie with letters delighted me. I wanted more, and she gave me a primer. It was easy to get the letters first; that was the way we learned to read. It was easy to get the words revealed in the letters. It was thrilling to follow the story the words put together. It was intriguing to solicit and be solicited by the ideas, the characters, the scenes and events of the story. It was natural and awe-inspiring to sense something palpable in the personage who had conceived the whole thing and written it down.

Thus began the wonderful adventure with books, in school, at home, in all sorts of circumstances. Sometimes I was encouraged, sometimes discouraged, but never stopped. The first book I picked up in babyhood was a friend. The book I have just laid down is a friend. My epitaph will be one statement at least: "He loved to read." To read was happiness.

But such happiness was not without tears. Mamma read for sheer joy, so easily and naturally that we were unaware of the long labor she toughed through to get at her books. Aunt Winnie loved to read, too, but her main concern with us in regard to reading was to teach us the business end of books. There was much gruelling spade work at the business end before we could enjoy freely the intellectual and aesthetic pleasures of reading. And there were tears of exasperation, never of defeat.

For me the bugaboo was arithmetic. It seemed straight-forward and generous to add, subtract, multiply, and divide whole numbers. But fractions seemed both confusing and picayunish. Why not, I felt, be generous and throw in the fractional parts? Problems seemed foolish: "I sold a pig for so much more than it would have cost me if, and if, and if..." Any pig raiser I knew and any pig buyer I knew had more common sense and understandable bases of trade. And partial payments! I loathed the system as corruption of business and character in real life, and as distortion of integrity in abstract school problems. I preferred cash, or fortitude to work and wait for things.

But the grind over arithmetic for me and over other hateful matters for others, according to their particular dislikes, was something to be endured by us and enforced by Aunt Winnie. There could be no fooling about this. We had to know and be sure. If not, backsides had to bear the sins of slow brains and weak wills. Aunt Winnie knew the moral roots of the intellectual life, and she dug around them and fertilized them well.

Home cultivated them, too. Home and school were one in recognizing the moral imperative. Each of us had home chores and school tasks from which there was no escape. The question, for example, was not: "Did the calves get fed and put up for the night?" It was: "Did Rob, whose duty it is, feed the calves and put them up?" I left them out one night because I relied on Travis' promise to put them up for me. One died from exposure. I cried and blamed Travis. But the fault remained fixed on me. Home made school seem practical. Papa and Uncle Charlie gave us actual exercises in arithmetic that were vital and interesting because they were necessary in work: toll to calculate on cotton, corn, and wheat; lumber to measure; pay rolls to calculate; tax-lists to add.

Work at the plow, at the shop, and at the sawmill nerved our muscles and brains. It made school seem restful in contrast. All the boys became competent farmers, carpenters, machinists, and lumbermen—not after school days but during school days. Papa even had them working as deputy sheriffs while they were yet in short pants.

I saw the older boys, brothers, cousins, and neighbors, now in school now out, as mature jobs called them.

They did not go to school and then go to work. They grew up in school and at work all together. Aunt Winnie supplied the steady book emphasis to each stage of their growing. They never graduated; they gradually matured. She was the formal, progressive, intellectual and moral stimulus in this system of home, work, and study which constituted the only Alma Mater they ever knew. The girls, Norman, Uncle Charlie's youngest son, and I, Papa's youngest son, were ultimately sent on to other schools. But it was only after we had won through to some competence in the home, school, and work situation. It was made possible by the superior competence of our elder brothers and cousins who never could be spared as we could be. Remembrance of my happiness in many years of school is with gratitude to them.

The highest moment in each day at home and school was for us to be told that chores and book-tasks were well enough done to allow free time for reading at will. We were all readers, some more so than others, but we were all inclined to play with books. We never in our childhood had anything that could be called a library. Later on Uncle Charlie did bring home from a sale two or three hundred leather-bound volumes of classics. But in the early, formative years, we simply

had a few random volumes. There was in school a
shelf containing, in addition to our textbooks, the
Holmes, the Barnes, and the Stickney readers, McCabe's
Pictorial History of the World, Anthon's *Classical Dictionary, Around the World in Eighty Days,* the Bible,
Foster's *Story of the Bible,* and a few of the Henty
books. There was on a stand Webster's *Unabridged
Dictionary.* These all we read, re-read, and leafed
through from the time when we could merely look at
the pictures till the time when we knew whole sections
of them by heart.

In the house there were dog-eared copies of Grimm,
Swiss Family Robinson, Arabian Nights, Andersen, all
with many pages missing. There were novels ranging
from *Little Women* to the thrillers of Mrs. E. D. E. N.
Southworth. Novels were our staple; we begged, bor-
rowed, and exchanged them.

We had *The News and Observer* and the *Christian
Advocate* from Raleigh. We tried to outwit each other
weekly so as to get first chance at the *Youth's Companion.* For a short while we took *McClure's Magazine.*
And we sneaked the magazine *Comfort* to read for-
bidden stories of "Jack Harkway out West among the
Indians." Mamma and I looked forward each month
to the arrival of the *Farm Journal.*

There were law books, some theological books, many reports and yearbooks, as from the Department of Agriculture, Turner's *North Carolina Almanac,* seed catalogues, and machinery catalogues. We read them all.

Mary and Helen went wild about *St. Elmo* and transcribed the love scene from it on the waiting room door at the Depot, so as never to be without its inspiration.

Greatly beloved, and free of cost, was Sears and Roebuck's catalogue. We read it and shopped in imagination. Moreover, we found news about books in its book section. I read about books there and made up ideal lists I would have bought if I could have got the money. I saved my pennies and gradually obtained *Alice's Adventures in Wonderland, Jo's Boys, Little Men, Eight Cousins, Scottish Chiefs,* and *Greek Heroes.* I don't know what we would have read if we could have got to the books. As it was, hunger for books made every morsel of print an Epicurean feast. This feeling for books was the great contribution of Aunt Winnie, a feeling pretty well implemented with ideas and information.

It was also a pleasure to be a part of the school family. Our main tasks were strictly individual—each one where he was, going as far as he could directly under Aunt Winnie. There were no classes, no examinations, no grades, no schedule, no promotion or demotion. She knew each one of us inside out. It was stimulating to see the whole field of knowledge spread out from a, b, to Virgil and Euclid, with each worker tending his own garden spot in it. But we had community concerns—Bible, prayers, songs; games of fox-in-the-wall, prisoner's base, stealing goods, round-cat, and basketball in the yard. Each day the whole school engaged in a spelling bee from the blue-back speller. On three Fridays each month we wrote "reproductive compositions"; Aunt Winnie would read to us some bit of history or literature, and we would reproduce it in our own words.

On every fourth Friday we wrote "original compositions," stories and essays right out of our own heads. The classic of these Fridays of pure literature was Harry's story of an entirely imaginary trip abroad. The high spot was the fare on the boat which took him across the ocean. "We had," he wrote, "butter and preserves for dinner every day."

But our happiness in the school family was not without tears. There was the matter of teasing. School was frank. A pupil in mental or moral arrears was cross-examined before highly curious and amused

hearers. No detail was too intimate to avoid full revelation. The sentiments in books moved me deeply. One
day my lesson was "Home Sweet Home." It made me
feel all the woes of an exile. I broke down and cried
when I stood up to read. Aunt Winnie asked bluntly.

"What are you crying for?"

I could not bring myself to reveal my sentiments
before my companions.

"I am crying because you made me stay in yesterday,"
I replied.

"Stay in again tomorrow!" commanded Aunt Winnie, with a slap on my ears that made them ring.

Aunt Winnie, though stern about crying complaints
such as I appeared to be making, would have understood about teasing. Papa and Uncle Charlie tormented
her to tears all the time about Uncle Sam, her beau.
And everyone teased everyone else. But I preferred
to cover up with a half-lie.

Soon thereafter I attempted to escape punishment by
telling a whole, blatant, senseless lie. I had scratched
the numeral "7" all over a song book in which I was
memorizing song number seven. It was an act of sub-
conscious doodling, but it looked like vandalism.

"Who did this?" demanded Aunt Winnie. Everybody knew that I had done it. But her attack embarrassed me.

"I don't know," I replied.

The book was forgotten in the presence of the lie. Aunt Winnie whipped me severely. Then she made Sallie write the word "Truth" on the blackboard in chalk and Joe write the word "Lie" on the wall in charcoal. Then, like Joshua, she cried to me, "Choose!" I did not quibble over "Truth" like "jesting Pilate"; I chose it sincerely. I hope it was written on my heart more permanently than it was on the blackboard. For somebody soon rubbed it off that. But "Lie" remained on the wall as the legend of my shame till the plastering fell.

"Who told that?" chuckled Grandma when she visited the school one day.

I could then smile, albeit sheepishly, and tell her that I had. A great philosopher has remarked that every experience of suffering makes two main appearances—first as tragedy, then as comedy. There were many tragic incidents in the experiences of all of us, now tamed by the years into gentler aspects.

We were used to whippings. Mamma and Aunt Lula wore out many a peachtree switch on us. Papa and Uncle Charlie seldom took a hand at whipping us except when we were in collective and open disturbance of the peace, as when we got to fighting on top of the house. Then they came up over the roof, one armed with a square, the other with a hand-saw. They spanked us without regard to whose child was being spanked, not so much for fighting as for our foolhardy choice of a battleground. We knew better than to challenge them.

But it was in our school traditions to challenge the teacher. Papa and Uncle Charlie told us sagas of their contests with their teacher. And Uncle Henry, from Six-Pound, told us of his struggles to outwit Grandpa, who was his teacher. He always stuffed his geography book in his pants as a protection against the inevitable whipping when his wits failed.

Whipping, which seemed so stupendous when it befell us, seems to me now a minor matter. The great remembrance stirs me to reverential gratitude. That is, of love equipped with keen intelligence and moral health. Aunt Winnie and our parents dug deep and laid solid foundations.

The tragedy, comedy, and commonplace of each school year wound up with a "Concert." We learned songs to sing and plays to act. Aunt Winnie was stage director. Aunt Lula was costume maker and scenery designer. Papa and Uncle Charlie executed all designs for scenery in the shop. We held the concert in the gin-house from which we removed temporarily the cotton-stalls. And when all was through we had ice cream.

On one commencement day two happenings threatened to break up our plans. The keyboard slipped out of the piano when it was being carried up a ramp into the gin-house, and broke over half of the pins to the hammers. And the railroad track buckled so in the heat that it appeared no train could pass. Our ice cream was to come on a train from Raleigh.

But Papa and Uncle Charlie took that piano into the shop and put new pins into the hammers before dark. The show went on!

Henry strutted in Grandma's shawl for a toga, brandished a sword of lath and a shield of tin, and told us, in the stentorian tones of a Roman soldier, "The night is black as the mother of Erebus." Ernest was a hit as an eccentric, deaf uncle. Joe and Charles were excruciatingly funny as black-face comedians. John and Harry, to their disgust, were fairies. One of the neighbor girls got her stage directions all mixed up with her lines, but she recited both with dramatic fire. Everybody had a part, was in good voice, and in fine histrionic mood. I was resplendent in silk as Little Boy Blue. But, worn out with the excitement of the day, I actually went to sleep on the hay and had to be prodded. I sprang up in confusion and could get but a weak "toot, toot" from my horn, on which I had hoped to blow the blast of a Roland.

The ice cream did come. It was abundantly eaten. And next day was vacation, dawning to the joyous clatter of the wheat harvest.

IV

Old Mary and I

THIS IS THE story of a gracious, gentle, and charming being—a lady of sterling character, fine intelligence, and adventurously imaginative spirit. She was one of my first and best teachers among many to whom I am sincerely grateful. She taught me responsibility for a job, reciprocity in relations, and resignation to our limitations, I think; at any rate, she was the means by which I learned them. She was an aristocrat with a proud lineage from the Island of Jersey, with a pedigree more selective than mine.

All this is true, even though she was nothing but a cow. I am wary of the expression, "nothing but." Who can define and delineate causation? Shakespeare says of one great formative influence in our lives: "The best in this kind are but shadows, and the worst are no worse if imagination do but amend them." Our spiritual life is all in one piece. Imagination is an aid to affection; affection is an aid to imagination. I grew to love Old Mary, for that was her name. But there was a time when I hated her. From hate to love is the story.

Old Mary was so important to us that anything concerning her welfare became a family problem. And Old Mary, herself, had introduced the problem by her spirit of adventure and her keen intelligence. She had learned how to take down the rail fence in the pasture and turn herself, the other cows, and the sheep into the corn and wheat. Moreover, there was a railroad which ran by our house. Old Mary might get killed.

Our elders went into conference, the whole six of them—Papa and Uncle Charlie, Mamma, Aunt Lula, Aunt Winnie and Grandma; the fifteen of us children swelled the proceedings with tumult and shoutings. A mandate emerged from the elders: Old Mary must stay in the lot where there wasn't a sprig of grass, and therefore one of the children must graze her each day, and twice a day, until she was filled. Papa and Uncle Charlie then left the conference, in sublime confidence that their mandate would be fulfilled. They dwelt on Olympus as twin Joves in our world, and had but to nod to be obeyed.

But the children and the women-folks locked in a

struggle of wills to determine which child should graze Old Mary. And, to my utter surprise and resentment, that child turned out to be me! I was to give several hours of my precious freedom each morning, and several each afternoon to the grazing business with Old Mary. Moreover, I was to feed her, milk her, and water her—to be her man-in-waiting, as it were.

I stood my ground with all the arguments my eight years of age could muster. But they were all brushed aside. No, Papa and Uncle Charlie could not build a new pasture fence of boards. This was an arresting thought to me. Could there be any limitations on the power of Papa and Uncle Charlie?

No, Arthur, Henry, Ernest, Joe, and Charles could not take care of a cow; they had more important things to do, on the farm, in the shop, at the sawmill. And as for Charles, lucky fellow, I knew myself that he, with an uncanny prescience, had pretended never to be able to learn to milk. No, John and Harry were not going to be called back to cow-grazing and milking. They had outgrown it, and were now good field hands. Of course, Sallie and Fannie were not going to have anything to do with such out-of-doors work; a woman's place was in the home. Hugh, Helen, Mary, and Norman were too little. In this I had some consolation. I was at least more important than somebody.

Grandma stayed aloof from our arguments and supplied the participants with peppermints. Mamma for once was adamant toward me. How, thought her cow-loving soul, could I fail to see the privilege of association with Old Mary? Aunt Lula murmured darkly that my bad disposition was coming to the fore again. Aunt Winnie said positively that it was time I learned to work.

This was another arresting thought. Was there an element of doing something one didn't want to do in this business of working? I thought I was working when I played with a seed-sower, strutting like Uncle Charlie, or pedalled the lathe in the machine shop and tried to get my hands good and black on the tools, like Papa's when he washed them for dinner. I thought everybody was doing what he pleased and that work was a dignified name for play.

Well, if I could not put off the impending job, I could experiment with mitigating it. Nobody could actually run away from a job in that family. I turned Old Mary out without a rope. She grazed a while in the clover patch and then made off for the railroad, the cornfield, and the woods beyond. I had given Old

Mary a set-up for her kind of fun; she didn't even have to take down a fence rail this time to get away to freedom. When I finally got her back in the lot, I was told in no uncertain terms that if I pulled this sort of stunt again, the well-known peach tree would be stripped of another keen switch. Our elders did not approach us by our intellectual ends alone.

I tried a rope, a short one. Old Mary grazed a while and then began to walk, then to trot, then with tail in the air, to gallop in sway-footed speed. When I had hung on till she was content to be led back, I tied her to a post, where nobody could see me, and gave her a beating. It was then she asserted the power of non-violence. She gazed at me with eyes of that limpid depth with which the goddess Hera shamed Zeus, the father of gods and men. I felt that I had profaned a communion that should be sacred.

I began to see Old Mary's point of view and to respect it. She had a will of her own and feelings of her own. Here she was shut off from the social joys of the cow community and confined to association with heartless me. I sought a mutual arrangement. I found that a rope, not too short and not too long, a quiet manner, and patient waiting would enable us both to stay in the clover patch in peace.

I tried a few experiments at shirking. I would appear in the fields with a hoe; but Uncle Charlie would run me back to Old Mary. I would busy myself with wood and water around the kitchen. The women-folks would accept the wood and water and then send me back to Old Mary. She would moo for me and when I would appear her voice would soften to a caress; she would lick me and seem to consider me as her calf. She had lost many calves, and her soul was deepened by grieving over them. She came to accept me as a symbol of all she had loved and lost.

Old Mary would graze and then lift her head and ruminate. I know not what impulses came to her from the sights and sounds of the other cows in the pasture. But, if she began to move toward them, she would feel the rope, and desist.

While I grazed her I read *Lena Rivers* and *English Orphans,* trash some would call them, spiritual memoirs to me. And I would muse in the summer peace. Bees would buzz, birds would sing, odors of flowers would thrill me. I would hear the children at play and see the men and boys companionable in the fields. But I would feel the rope in my hands and make myself content.

As I would lift my head and look away in reverie, I would sometimes catch Old Mary's eye, veiled like mine in contemplation. As our glances met, I seemed to feel a bond of the spirit, transcending the physical bond of the rope which united boyhood and cowhood.

V.   Oh, How Sweet To Walk

§1

> "Oh, how sweet to walk
> In this pilgrim way,
> Leaning on the Everlasting Arms."

THUS WE ALL sang together in Sunday School at old Calvary Church, built by our grandfather and his neighbors, Methodists, and proud to be. Aunt Lula pumped away and played the organ, no mean achievement, with her feet having to pedal in one rhythm and her hands to play in another. Uncle Charlie sang a good, accurate bass out of the corner of his mouth, which marked the time and held all the singing together. Some of the women and girls sang full, melodious sopranos and altos. Some of the men and boys sang competent baritones and tenors. Others of us experimented, now with reedy tenors, now with bullfrog basses, now with the air. One, his soul caught up in ecstasy, went his own gait in a determined baritone, exactly one measure behind the rest. We children interpreted the grand hymn "Hallelujah, Thine the Glory" to be a song of invitation, "Hallelujah, Jine the Chorus," and "jine" it we did with a will. Truly we made a joyful noise unto the Lord.

Then would follow a simple, direct, humble prayer to our Heavenly Father, led by Mr. Tom Myrick, the superintendent, or Mr. Jack King, the assistant superintendent. It was a gentle, appealing exercise of dignity and trust. The secretary would call the roll. The patriarchs and elder mothers of the church were not on the rolls of Sunday School, which was run by the middle-aged and young parents and the youths, maidens, and children. Each name as it was called brought up the image of a neighbor known and loved, and most of the children were our schoolmates. Few failed to answer "Present." There was another rousing song and then we separated into classes here and there in the one-room building.

Uncle Charlie put the grown folks through the exercises in the Adult Quarterly. The Quarterly left nothing to chance. It presented a bit of Scripture, commented on it briefly, analyzed the whole into simple questions, and printed out the desired answers. Cousin Alla took the intermediate group through their Quarterly in much the same manner. There were two younger classes of boys and girls, each with lesson leaflets. Cousin Eddie took the youngest boys through the Catechism. He dispensed with literature altogether and went through rapid-fire questions to which we shot back the answers:

"Who made you?" ... "God."

"Who was the first man?" ... "Adam."

"Who was the oldest man?"

At this question John raised his hand in eager assertion of knowledge. "Mr. Albert Shaw," he replied.

Mr. Albert Shaw was indeed the oldest man we knew anything about. He and his three sons were close to us, kindly neighbors and sources of scuppernong grapes and watermelons. Also, to speak in Biblical style, we had our First Kings and our Second Kings. First Kings were Mr. Tom King and his family. They gave us the best clear-seed peaches that were ever grown, and the boys were our guides to nature. Their woodcraft and their pioneer skills would have aroused the envy of Daniel Boone himself. Second Kings were Mr. Fab King and his family, nearly grown, jolly men. I treasured my first knife, given to me by Whit King, though I nearly cut my finger off with it. And I had ridden to their home on Blake's back and had gloated over the most complete farm I had ever seen. Blake promised me the colt which was tottering around as on stilts in the barnyard, provided

the colt would follow me home. He never would. I
had sensed there a deep reverence as the strapping boys
gathered around their father for Bible reading and
prayers at bed-time. And all the other neighbors we
knew intimately and loved. School and Sunday School
joined us together.

There were several songs after the lessons, then the
unvarying formula of dismissal from Mr. Myrick:
"Consider yourselves dismissed."

Our "pilgrim way" to and from Sunday School was
a journey of three miles, which we traveled in a hack.
Neighbors would come out of their gates in buggies,
wagons, or on horseback, and join the procession as
it moved up. They would all start with us in full procession on the trip back and leave us one by one as
their gates were reached again. Skinner Pearson would
ride cross-wise on his horse, make faces at us, and otherwise entertain us until he reached the woods path at
White's Cut which led him across the railroad to his
home. Our road led by the water tank on the railroad.
This spot on the top of the hill was called "Summit."
We took it literally to mean the very top of the world.
And the railroad suggested far parts, for close by on a
telegraph pole was a sign "Atlanta: 511 miles." We
would plague Uncle Charlie all the way home to be

allowed to go barefooted after dinner. For Sunday
School was mostly a warm-weather affair.

Our journeys to Sunday School and our schedule of
"taking-in" were both leisurely. We went by sun time.
The men would visit, discuss crops and politics, and
whittle under a great oak on the church grounds. The
women would gossip and talk about households, children, and fashion, in the pews. We children would
romp and wrestle or call up doodle bugs from their
conical holes in the sand under the oaks. Only when
the last buggy or wagon straggled in would the organ
sound to summon us to begin. It was all a neighborhood affair, distinct from "church" and the ministra-
tion of the preacher. The preacher was busy for three
Sundays each month at other churches on his circuit.

It was a sweet, reassuring sentiment to feel beneath
us the strong arms of God, seemingly one with the
warm, loving arms of parents and neighbors. Home,
neighborhood, week-day school and Sunday School,
joined hands in easy harmony. Aunt Winnie saw to
it that we learned our sacred lessons as zealously as we
did our secular ones. She encouraged us to read the
Bible, not only as the literal word of God, but for fun
as the most entertaining book ever written. She per-
suaded us to memorize some of its chapters for fun;

she allowed us to memorize others as substitute for more drastic punishment when we committed minor offenses. Thus were we made familiar with great characters, great stories, great images, great ideas, with the real epic and formative influence of our race and nation.

We saw in Abraham the type of parental sternness, discipline, and affection. We adventured and played in the spirit of David. We gave rein to spiritual passion with Isaiah. We found in the Psalms the expression of our own pastoral. Proverbs seemed echoes of shrewd, salty humor and sense we heard every day from both whites and Negroes.

The Negroes were always making Biblical allusions. Aunt Mimy said that Miss Sallie in her wedding dress looked like the "Queen of 'Shebbidy.'" Nancy laughed heartily at this and explained to us that Aunt Mimy didn't really know. She had meant, said Nancy, to refer to the "Queen of 'Shevy.'" Gentle-souled, devout, old Henry Falcon, with whom I carpentered, piously did his work, remembering the Great Carpenter. He called me "Good Shepherd" because I looked after the sheep. I felt like a good shepherd when the sheep remained quietly in the pasture. But when, as often happened on the muddiest of days, they got into the wheat,

I felt like one of the more pessimistic minor prophets.

We sang hymns and Sunday School songs with gusto in school and around the piano in the parlor. We said our prayers morning and night.

We said grace at each meal. All things at home, in the neighborhood, at school, and at Sunday School taught us to lean with joy and trust on the Everlasting Arms.

§2

On one Sunday in each month the preacher came and we would stay after Sunday School for "Church." The preachers came and went according to the will of the Bishop, whom we never saw, and the influence of the Presiding Elder, who came every now and then to a session, mysterious to us, Quarterly Conference. But we took pride in the look of religious statesmanship on Uncle Charlie's face when Quarterly Conference came around. We felt sure things went well with him there. We also felt that his going to it made the Church a part of our business. We regarded ourselves as members of the Church, and the Church as a member of us.

Church services were more than Sunday School, but not so interesting because we did not feel the same sense of participation in them. But we sat patiently through them and enjoyed the concourse of people. Clothes were finer than in Sunday School, more rustly and dignified. All the patriarchs and elder mothers of the congregation then appeared in their best. We pricked up our ears and felt a sense of participation when they took part. Two of the patriarchs were Cousin John and Cousin Randall. Cousin John could pray in public with eloquence and deep emotional power. Cousin Randall spoke not at all in public. One Sunday the preacher, being new, called on Cousin Randall to lead in prayer. Cousin Randall spoke out so that all could hear:

"John, you pray. You can put up a much better prayer than I can."

And John did pray.

The preachers varied in personal, mental, and spiritual qualities, from the white-haired and prophet-like Mr. Hermon, of whom I was mortally afraid because he jokingly threatened to put me in the pulpit and make me preach—on through the quiet and scholarly Mr. Davis, to the gentle, English, Mr. Goodchild, with his Yankee wife and precisely-spoken but delightful little girl, Gwendolyn. Of all the preachers the greatest by common consent was the large-minded, imperious-souled Doctor Burton, whose name I bear. Our district was his home, and not even the Bishop dared to send him away from it. One of them, a saint and a scholar, Doctor Bumpas, could fill the church with light and warmth. He had about him the full flavor of consecrated work, letters, and wise urbanity, seasoned with country wisdom.

But all the preachers entered with ease and quickness the homes and spirit of the neighborhood and joined them in the spirit of the Church. They had about them the air of mountain peaks. They were concentrated on great thoughts, great dogmas, great purposes. We could sense these by their tone and manner in the pulpit. Sometimes they bore down a little heavy on dancing and cards, our Rook, Setback, and Five Hundred, particularly when Aunt Lula's brother, Uncle Johnnie, and his wife, Aunt Bettie, came on their Summer visits from Baltimore. We loved to dance the square dance to fiddle and banjo. I don't think the preachers worried very deeply over these sins of ours except in the reforming zeal of the August revival. But if they ever got us worked up in August to give them up, we always backslid by Christmas. We were Methodists; we believed in backsliding; and, as an old Negro said, "Praise God, we practiced it." As to liquor, we were at one with the preachers, though liquor was all around us. We had one acquaintance who got both himself and his horse drunk every Saturday and rode through the neighborhood like a Bacchanalian Centaur.

The preacher usually carried a little black satchel full of books and notes, with a clean shirt tucked in. We always expected the preacher to come to our house for a long visit, and he always came. Papa once essayed to help a strange preacher with his bag.

"What on earth have you got in this to make it so heavy?" he asked by way of conversation.

The visitor drew himself up pompously.

"Theology! Theology!" he replied.

"You seem to have more of it in your satchel than in your head," rejoined Papa, nettled by a pose so uncharacteristic of the preachers we knew.

At home with us the preacher never suggested so much the business of preaching. He was a stimulus to elevated conversation. The dinner table became a symposium of religious thought and affairs in the light of religious thought. We children who had to wait, because there were but ten places at the first table, listened with interest unless the wait became too long.

"Are you gentlemen going to eat all day?" Fannie once asked. She broke up the protracted session. In the winter the circle around the fire in the parlor became a forum. In the summer we sat on the front porch, our nerves soothed by the lush air of twilight.

We even learned to act naturally about family prayers when the preacher came, though the ceremony was unusual with us when no preacher was there. Mamma would ring the bell as for breakfast. We would come on the run, and she would shoo us into the parlor. We would listen to some beautiful passage, read in a husky, morning voice. Then we would kneel, facing our chairs, and peep through our fingers while the preacher prayed.

In the front hall was a closet with an alcove leading to it. In the closet were stored sugar, cakes, preserves, and pickles. We used to raid the stores, and Grandma would waylay us with the broom. One day she came down on some fancied marauder with broom handle. It was the new preacher who had gone into the alcove to get his overshoes.

§3

The annual revival meeting raised a question in our minds that home, school, Sunday School, and Church proper never put to us in any direct way; were we entitled to walk in the "pilgrim way" at all, or to be

sure of the Everlasting Arms without definite conviction of sin, conversion, open confession, and, desirably,
formal union with the Church? The revival was called
"Big Meeting" and it came each year in August when
the crops were laid by—a Pentecost called by the cal-
endar, as it were.

In all things other than the Church and the com-
missariat, it was a time of profound worklessness. Not
a hoe or a plow stirred on the farms; not a wheel
turned at shop or mill while the great question was
being put. The bustle of a train passing by seemed a
blatant interruption. Some might stay away; they were
few in number. Almost everybody went to the Church,
every day for at least a week, sometimes two weeks.
There were two services each day with dinner on the
grounds.

Nancy, Aunt Mimy, and Aunt Becky would come
to help Sarah in the kitchen. John and Harry would
run the dog, Rex, into a delirium catching chickens to
be killed, picked, and fried. Travis would make havoc
among the lambs. Old hams would come down from
their nails in the smokehouse. Bushels of corn would
go into puddings, and all the vegetables into Brunswick
stews. Biscuits by the gross and the great gross were
baked. Cakes, pickles, and preserves were added by the

dozens or the gallons respectively. Baskets, cracker-boxes of the old kind, each about the size of a steamer trunk, were packed. It was not only a time for the family to turn out full strength, but each family augmented with all the far-away members returned for a reunion, and with company to the capacity of every bed and pallet in the house. For like preparations went on in all the homes of the neighborhood. It was also a season of community open-house for all comers. Each housewife would have felt humiliated if one visitor went unfed. And each housewife was on parade as a good provider.

Sometimes the preacher while he was in the pulpit would urge the providers to bring "just a crust" so as not to impede the Spirit. But this same preacher at the table under the trees would more than likely say, also:

"My, my, such delectable lamb! Did you make this cake? I think I'll take just a little more of that ham!" For the preacher knew that working men deserve to eat. And, make no doubt of it, all present were in travail.

Nobody ever got away with trying to make Big Meeting nothing but a picnic. The deadly seriousness of its purpose weighed on all despite the festive and picnicky appearance of the tables at recess hour, the couples spooning in buggies, the flirting with fans, the matronly jaunts of women to the woods on one side of the Church, the jovial saunters of men to those on the other. Morning merely began the pressure, recess was a suspension of it. All too soon the organ would sound, and the "workers" would eye the sinners over their turkey wing fans. These workers were heroic in their zeal. Few of the congregation could bring themselves to appeal to the sinners. Even the regular preacher took second rank at the revival. The intimate probing of souls required a specialist visitor, the Revivalist.

The Revivalists were earnest and consecrated men, masters in the psychology of emotional appeal. Some were thunderers from Sinai. Some sang songs of Mother, Home, and Heaven. Some were sweetly reasonable and persuasive. But all of them knew how to sift the congregation and single out the unsaved. Many years of camp-meeting tradition made the method sacred. First, there would be a call for the saved to gather for thanksgiving at the altar. This was when the true saints would shout in joyous abandon, though some would look self-conscious at the temerity of their assurance. Then would come a call for all Church members who felt the need of refreshing to come. This would use up one day. Then at each service thereafter the argument, the persuasion from the pulpit, and the pleas of individual workers would concentrate on the unsaved to get them to shake hands with the preacher, to kneel at the altar, to pray, to rise and acknowledge conversion. Emotionalism made fantastic happenings, but never comedy. It was a high and serious, direct attack on the resources of the spirit.

We granted the arguments without question. We acknowledged our conviction of sin. We responded inwardly to every persuasion. We felt no sense of strangeness at the time or the method. We wanted to express our repentance in the accepted way. What held us back was embarrassment. We could not bring ourselves easily to step out before all those people. All the naturalness and joy of Sunday School and Church seemed as in another world. The ordeal was torture. But, torture or not, that was the accepted way. That was the way we accepted.

But not without long waiting, long interior debate. That is why the dinner hour was bitter-sweet. Travis, the mules, the trees, the sunshine, seemed bits of reality seen through a mist. And the food, though excellent, was eaten in abstraction. I have never since those days eaten sweet pickle and fried chicken together without a return of "the conviction of sin."

VI.   Not Without Sweat

IN THE SUMMER, when I was 10 years old, Uncle Charlie put me to work driving Fleetfoot, the horse who pulled a lumber truck at the sawmill. Eight-year-old Hugh had to help me by driving every other trip. Twelve-year-old John and Harry had to make every trip, and load and unload lumber all day long. All the older boys worked here and there at the sawmill. And Uncle Charlie had to saw, as well as supervise the whole process of lumbering from stump to box-car. But I had no sympathy for any of these. I resented the interruption to my researches in Swiss Family Robinson and related documents and projects.

For I was engaged in planning an ideal way of life, which was to go on a voyage with all the family and get ship-wrecked on some appropriate tropical strand. I was seeking in the atlas some proper place. And from the pages of Sears and Roebuck's catalogue I was selecting better implements and supplies than were on the ship which carried the family Robinson.

As a secondary project I was contemplating farming. My vision of the proper way to farm was made up of my love of its pastoral scenes, my sympathy with Mamma's love of the farm, and much reading in the yearbook of the Department of Agriculture, the *International Stockbook*, Sears and Roebuck's catalogue, the seed catalogues of T. W. Wood and Sons of Richmond, and *The Farm Journal*. This last was the special bond of professional reading between Mamma and me. It was complete with reference to all departments of farming, and it was inspirational with an essay each month by Judge Jacob Biggle on "High Farming at Elmwood."

My views as to high farming at Edgewood, our home, was a compound of Negro hands to do the dirty work, self-operating machinery from the catalogue, crops as in the seed catalogue and yearbook, and animals as in the stockbook. They provided me plenty of leisure to read by the fire in winter and on the porch in summer. About real work, I was like George, the young mule, who protested and groaned at the plow and lay down to rest in the furrow when he got tired. I learned a lot about vacations from George.

I did not love the sawmill. It was raucous, and its effects on the country-side were ugly. I loved the log-woods with the chop of the axe, the clang of the saw, the shout of the lumbermen as the the great trees fell; and I loved the oxen and mules which drew the logs out. But Old Bill, the patriarch of the logging mules, had given me an inferiority complex about log-woods. He respected only his driver, Horace. I had undertaken to drive him. He looked around, sneered at me, and took charge of the wagon himself, just as though I had been merely a gnat. Moreover, I resented the gradual encroachment of the sawmill on farming. I feared that Uncle Charlie was losing his interest in our play on the farm, which had been our chief activity. In fact, it seemed to me that play had gone out of the world.

But Fleetfoot! Who could fail to sympathize with that lovable horse? He and Step-light were heroes to us because they had been colts when Papa and Uncle Charlie were just on the verge of manhood; and here they were, each in his prime when, as we thought in the usual distorted perspective of youth about the age of its elders, Papa and Uncle Charlie were old men. They were brothers like Papa and Uncle Charlie, and their respective temperaments reminded us of these two brothers. Step-light maintained a quiet, dignified remoteness from our concerns, and was irascible if we bothered him. He would make as if to bite us when we ran by his stall, but would snap his teeth just short of us. He would chase us up into apple trees in the orchard if we teased him, and then pretend to graze; but he would always keep an eye on us until somebody came to drive him off.

Papa, as sheriff and "outside man of affairs," was somewhat remote from our daily affairs because he was gone from home a good deal. We attributed his pre-occupation with outside concerns to temperamental aloofness. But at the same time we were conscious of his close regard of us, like that of Step-light, keeping us up the tree. And, like Step-light, he was at times belli-cose, but never actually dangerous. The good-natured slowness and inefficiency of many of the Negroes ex-asperated him to a pitch of temper. But the Negroes understood him. They would whisper to each other, "You better look out; the Sheriff's spitting cotton this morning," referring to Papa's habit of expectorating freely when he was angry.

Fleetfoot, like Uncle Charlie, was our playmate and companion. He was warm and intimate in disposition and would seem to smile when he saw us coming. He seemed to enjoy the liberties we took with him, such as crawling all over him and all under him, pulling his tail and his mane. He would come up to us and nudge us to make us play with him. I feared that hard work at the sawmill would dampen Fleetfoot's spirits.

But, on the contrary, he was magnificent at work. No matter what the size of the load, Fleetfoot would arch his compact little frame, dig his feet into the ground, and pull it. He triumphed in his energy. But he never got too tired to play. Even though he might be dripping with sweat he would nudge me for a romp. And on holidays he would amuse himself by teasing the mules in the lot. He would catch one by the tail, close up at the rump, and drive him around by the hour. Then, as if to make amends, he would pull the pin out of the lot gate and turn all the mules out and lead them for a run.

Sympathy with Fleetfoot led me to observe more closely Uncle Charlie and the boys, and also the Negroes. I saw a splendid and untiring competence in their working. I did not as yet participate in this. The mill moved on here and there to various stations nearer the woods, and they went with it. I was put back to the farm, the shop, and the gin. But I observed them in my special function as dinner-carrier. I had to go each

day to take them tin buckets full of hot food. In my
haste one day I stumped my toe on a root in the path,
fell, and spilled the dinner. Luckily I fell in dry sand
and the dinner was fried chicken. I brushed it off on
my pants, put it back into the buckets, and was never
found out.

But I especially observed at this period their ex-
uberant energy for play, with Uncle Charlie still the
playmate, and leader. All during the dinner hour, and
also when some stoppage occurred about the mill, they
played—wrestling, boxing, lifting. One man would
over-power another and hold him while another
spanked him with a board; this was called "bucking."
Or one man would throw another, partially strip him
and hold him while the fireman poured oil over his
anatomy; this was called "greasing."

I was pretty good at running and at "acting" on a
horizontal bar. But I was no good in these feats of
strength. I was crushed by June's remark:

"Little boy, don't your legs whistle in March?"

Baseball was their obsession in spring and summer.
They would work until near sundown and then practice until it was dark. And on Saturdays they would
play match games. Uncle Charlie loved to encourage
them. He had played baseball when nobody had worn

a mitt or a glove. I was a literary player, in that I knew by heart all the records in both the Reach and the Spalding guides. And I tried to play. I imagined the impact of ball on bat but I usually struck out. I crouched in fancy for a quick play at short-stop, but the ball usually went on between my legs. I judged the flies and poised for a peg to the plate, but ended my dream by chasing the ball into the bush. I was the sort of player they used when nobody else could be found. My souvenir of baseball is a bridge replacing three front teeth.

Hunting was their passion in fall and winter. Not fox-hunting or 'possum hunting, and only occasionally a turkey or a goose. It was bird-hunting—the swish of corduroy or duck pants through the bushes and the broom straw, the dogs circling and quartering. The point, with dogs and men frozen like statues in the fields. The boom of wings, the bang of guns, the pant and snuffle of retrievers, the leisurely round-up of single birds. No day was too unseasonable for them to go out. It was their dream when they worked, their talk till bed-time. And they were masters at it.

I tried to hunt—sparrows with an air rifle. I would shoot, miss, and see the sparrows fly away. But one day a sparrow seemed to be hypnotized by my efforts. He sat on a limb by the stable. I shot and missed, re-loaded, shot and missed, re-loaded, shot, and hit him in the throat. When he fell, all my zeal to hunt fell with him. My total bag to date is one sparrow, five quail, and one goose.

When, long afterward, I went to war, the boys wanted to know if I would shoot at the enemy or read at 'em. As a matter of fact, I shot but once, and that was through a harmless confusion of orders. But I did my best reading in a dugout—the Bible, The Oxford Book of English Verse, and Charles Van Loan's golf stories in the Saturday Evening Post.

"Mary had a little lamb," sang Uncle Johnny. He would repeat this line over and over at the top of his voice. In between he would whistle a tune of two or three bars. And, as he sang and whistled, he would squint along the lines of a cider press he was making against a great oak tree. He was an expert with tools, and the press rapidly took shape under his hand. All of his being was concentrated on his work; the singing and whistling were mere overflows of his artistic energy. For he was an artist and endowed each job of work with distinction and beauty. He fascinated me and I would spend the whole day watching him and listening to him.

"Mary had a little lamb," he sang out for perhaps the hundredth time. Then he suddenly straightened up from his work and poked me in the side with his finger. "Ha, Rob, it took Mary a long time to have that lamb, didn't it? You want to know why I sing and whistle so much? Well, ever since I was at Fort Fisher my ears have been ringing. They were injured by the guns, and the more noise I make, the less I hear the ringing." I still refuse to think that diversion of attention was his sole object in singing and whistling. He loved music, though his music ran mostly to noise. And he adored noise. He shouted with abandon and greeted his neighbor each morning with a "Good morning, Sam" that carried easily over the quarter of a mile that separated them. And when he sneezed the reverberations echoed over a mile of hill and woods. When he was amused he both laughed and shouted, and the sound of his joy seemed to fill a township. He seemed to inspire noisy response. Though my own house was nearly a half mile away, I could hear him greet his horse in the morning and hear old Dan's whicker of delight. He was the soul of kindness to his farm animals and achieved comradeship with them.

In fact he was in intimate communion with all things. Sometimes he carried this intimacy to the point of danger. He observed a buzz saw in the wood-shop one morning. It seemed to be neither running nor standing still. He touched it and cut off the tip of his finger. He exploded with laughter at this joke on himself. A few

days later he returned to the shop, still full of amuse-
ment at his folly, and sought to explain his accident.
"Why, the damned thing seemed to be as still as it is
now," he said, and touched the saw again. It took another piece off his finger. This was the finger with
which he poked me in the side. The nail of it had
grown back like a shoe button right on the tip.

The intrepid and impulsive spirit of Uncle Johnny
seemed to invite ridiculous and dangerous things to
happen to him. He found a hollow log and decided
to fill it with gun-powder for a Christmas firecracker.
He prepared the gigantic instrument with great skill,
laid it in the barnyard, lit the fuse, and sat on the fence
to watch it go off. He shouted with glee at the noise
and power. He had a tremendous ram, known to be
dangerous. But he forgot about the animal as he
stooped to pick up trash in the barn-yard. The ram attacked him in the rear and nearly drove his spine
through his skull. Uncle Johnny rejoiced in the prowess
of his ram.

When he was seventy-two years old Uncle Johnny
went into the pasture and was attacked by a young bull.
He was knocked down by the bull's rush, but he got
the animal by the horns, held his body between them
so that he could not be gored, and shouted for help.

His wife came with a fence rail and gave the bull such a beating that he was glad to get free and flee to the back side of the pasture. Uncle Johnny felt no rancor toward the bull.

While Uncle Johnny looked on such happenings as all in the day's work and play, Papa and Uncle Charlie deplored them and used them to point a moral: namely, that Uncle Johnny ought to have more sense. Uncle Johnny heard them with humorous tolerance, but with no promise toward reform. In fact, he was never interested in reform, except in one particular: he quit using tobacco. Papa and Uncle Charlie would grant him no moral superiority in this. They claimed that he took more pleasure in bragging to them about his will power than he did in smoking and chewing tobacco.

But, if Papa or Uncle Charlie were careless or foolish and came to grief, Uncle Johnny gave them a sympathy unpolluted by preachments. Uncle Charlie in cutting up a hog made a mis-stroke and cut his finger to the bone. He was telling Uncle Johnny how it happened.

"I was cutting away," said Uncle Charlie.

"A-a-h!" sighed Uncle Johnny in anticipation of impending catastrophe.

"And I didn't notice where my finger was," continued Uncle Charlie.

"Phoot, phoot, phoot," ejaculated Uncle Johnny.

"When, all of a sudden the knife...!"

"Oh, dammit to hell! Charlie, dammit to hell!" shouted Uncle Johnny in an agony of compassion.

Uncle Johnny didn't know that he was swearing. His thoughts and intents were pure. His profanity was a sub-conscious result of army life.

"Why, dammit, Sir," he said to the minister, "I wouldn't have cussed in your presence if I had known you were a preacher."

With Uncle Johnny, to think was to act with all the concentration of his being. He never got but one idea at a time. He was artistic in executing this idea. But he never tried to get one thing in relation to another. He got interested in raising fine dogs for sale, and kept them in the yard. Then he got interested in raising sheep, and built up a fine flock in the pasture. His dogs, run wild through neglect, killed his sheep one Sunday morning. Uncle Johnny killed his dogs and went out of both businesses that same day.

His life was a series of decided entrances into this business or that, followed by equally decided exits. He invented a fine churn-power, became convinced that the manufacture of it would be a good business and spent hundreds of dollars on tools and materials, including five hundred dollars worth of coiled steel springs. He made two sample churn-powers, placed them in a wagon, and set out to take orders for them in the country. The response to his salesmanship was so discouraging that in one day he gave up the whole venture. His next step was to throw the steel springs in a bonfire, straighten them out, and use the wire for the most expensive grape arbor the country had ever seen.

The grapes, however, were a great success, and Uncle Johnny became a wine-maker. But about this time prohibition regulations began to impede the wine business. Uncle Johnny immediately plowed up every grapevine on the place.

He had experimented in his youth with tobacco farming in Granville County. But in his mature years he returned to a three-hundred-acre farm he had inherited from his father. Amid a series of economic extravaganzas he kept ever afterwards to one line of livelihood—a garden farm which he cultivated himself with old Dan. His garden was superlative in the neighborhood for earliness, quality, and generosity. The finest of all the choice fruits and vegetables which we enjoyed at home, except watermelons from Mr. Tom Shaw, we got as a gift from Uncle Johnny. In return Papa and Uncle Charlie gave him the freedom of the tools, machinery, and materials in the shop.

Outside this competent system of subsistence farming

he used his land as a playground; which is to say that, while he did not despise money, he engaged in making a cotton crop, in logging, or wood-cutting as employments undertaken for pure zest in country enterprises. He loved to invent new tools and methods of cultivation and to try them out. When his experimental fervor was exhausted for the time being he would abandon the crop. He would invent a new type of log cart, a new method of loading, and make these signals for a forest enterprise.

Then he would turn from cropping and lumbering altogether, and spend a year or two fishing in Roanoke River with excellent fish-traps of his own invention. On the place were barns erected in a tobacco experiment, but long since abandoned, a chicken house of colossal proportions which had not held his interest over a year, and a goat-proof fence of no more ultimate use than to hold his one milk-cow. It was a delight to me just to stay around a man who played at his work so interestingly and who surrounded his experiments with such broad margins of time, space, and economic freedom.

I have seen many partial amateurs. But Uncle Johnny was the only complete amateur I ever had a chance to observe intimately. He was completely free and completely self-contained. He was never bored for a moment. Life was a perpetual game with him. He never sought a thrill. He carried his thrill with him into every operation. His energies, his aspirations, and his circumstances were one full current. Gusto is the word that expresses him. He tasted life fully.

I was raised on the novels of Thomas Nelson Page and of Mary Johnston, histories and biographies of the Confederacy, the romanticism of the South. What I was looking for in the flesh was a hero of the War to act the conventional part and to speak the appropriate lines. Here was Uncle Johnny. I knew that he had enlisted by special permission on account of his youth and had got up from typhoid fever to fight with distinction at Fort Fisher, had endured imprisonment at Elmira, N. Y., had suffered a relapse into fever, and had tramped home after his release. I expected him to play the part for me. But he refused to attitudinize. Historically he considered the war to be a damn-fool affair. And personally he reduced it to still smaller proportions, an incident in his boyhood. He never defended it or, for that matter, discussed it. It was simply part of a life too full to be fixed in one tragic image. He had merely taken it and all its consequences in his stride.

He bore no ill will for the North. On one occasion he met a man who had fought on the Union side at Fort Fisher. The two of them joked and laughed over the affair with the emotional detachment of chess-players analyzing a finished game. In fact, Uncle Johnny was unusually national in his tastes for so sectional an atmosphere. In his library I could find the national magazines, the New York papers, in particular the *World's Work*. And his home was a meeting place of hunters from the North.

Uncle Johnny was pure in his intentions and without guile in his dealings with others. He expected a reciprocal spirit from others. Usually he was not disappointed. But on one occasion he was discussing a consignment of fruit trees with a nursery agent. He pointed out that the trees were not what he had ordered. The nurseryman insisted that they were and then began to intimate that Uncle Johnny was not exactly candid in his statement. It took a few moments for Uncle Johnny to catch the saleman's drift. Then he dashed his spectacles to the ground and reached for the salesman. But the salesman had got Uncle Johnny's purpose while it was forming. He was a hundred yards away before Uncle Johnny's spectacles reached the ground.

When Uncle Johnny came to live on his farm just up the road and across the railroad from us, his three sons, Tom, Henry, and Lyman, were grown men who worked elsewhere than at home. Uncle Johnny with his wife, quiet, little invalid, Aunt Fannie, lived alone, except for Aunt Bettie, his sister who lived with them until after Grandma died, when she came to spend the remainder of her days with us. Aunt Bettie was just the opposite of Uncle Johnny, except in one particular. Like him she loved to shout and sing occasionally. She had the urge of high ideals with no will at all to execute any of them and no grace of persuading others. It made her life a Cassandra-like existence! "This ought to be done. That ought to be done." She was the abstract imperative. She kept to her room except at meal times. Nobody ever paid any attention to her observations on what ought to be done. Uncle Johnny would murmur, "Ah, Bet!...Ah, Bet!" Our elders at home simply remained silent.

From the time of Great Aunt Mary there had been some such stubborn, but abstracted, personality in the family. Great Aunt Mary had gone her way in deafness and obstinacy, taking a daily walk on the railroad track until a train hit her and killed her. Aunt Bettie never walked. She just sat. But she lived to be eighty-six years of age. For every day of these years she said somebody ought to do this or that.

Uncle Johnny never said anybody ought to do anything. He just simply did what he pleased in entire competence to handle his own affairs and let other people handle theirs. He, with Uncle Idy, and Uncle Tommy who died in the War, and Great Uncle Jim who survived the War with him, along with Aunt Jennie whom we saw occasionally on visits from her home in Richmond, and many more whom the years had taken, constituted the older set in Papa's and Uncle Charlie's family. Papa and Uncle Charlie were younger sons by Grandpa's second marriage. With Grandma they had inherited the home place. They were not amateurs in work like Uncle Johnny. Though their occupations varied, their attitude was sternly professional.

It was exhilarating to observe the play spirit of Uncle Johnny. He achieved a wonderful personal adventure with huge enjoyment to himself, and with pleasure for all who were his relatives and neighbors.

Uncle Johnny in every attitude was a Christian. But he was independent and unconventional. He took no part in Church membership and affairs. When the revivals used to reach a high pitch of enthusiasm, the minister would go to see Uncle Johnny and try his hand on him. Uncle Johnny remained polite but independent.

"Pshaw! Pshaw!" he would murmur. "I read the Bible. It says the Kingdom of Heaven is within you."

WHEN WE WENT down to the Depot to see the trains pass, we felt an elation kin to that of Doctor Johnson when he surveyed the variety of human life in London. The railroad brought drama and pageantry into our lives. Just as English boys are said to learn geography from the names and routes of ships, we learned the great routes of a continent from names of railroads on the box cars. Every variety of occupation and pleasure seemed to pass before us as passengers came and went, all pausing at the station for leisurely talks. They made the waiting room a sort of cultural forum. One of my first impulses toward Greek came from Mr. Tom Mason as he waited for the train and discussed languages with the postmaster, Mr. Ashley Wilkins. Mr. Wilkins was a devoted scholar, using six foreign languages and possessing two University degrees. Mr. Nick Wilkins, brother to Ashley, was a dreamer about the possibilities of power in the Roanoke Falls. He kept civil engineers coming and going constantly on his many surveys of the river.

Jim Benn, the station master, was our host at the station, our oracle, and our news commentator. He got news tips hot off the wires and told them to us long before they appeared in the newspapers.

The conductor of the local freight was a philosopher. "My father left me," he said, "exactly what God gave a billy goat: a hard head and a clear conscience. All a man needs is to be able to take what comes and to have nothing to be ashamed of." All the railroad men had about them the same air of adventure which today we associate with aviators. I have not seen a more dignified professional competence than that displayed by Mr. Pendleton, an engineer who saluted us daily as he passed the house. Nor have I seen greater aplomb than that possessed by Captain Cain, one of the passenger train conductors. He combined the qualities of a military commander with the perfect voice of an orator. Since Arthur was for a long time an engineer, we felt a sense of ownership in the railroad, and competence to discuss any railroad problem from a valve gear to a general strike.

Hunters from the North would come and go with

their dogs and guns and their precious strings of quail.
Exotic-looking and sounding passengers would pick
bolls of cotton from our lower lot sometimes when the
train stalled by it, and smell them as though they were
flowers. Mr. Bronson, a learned Episcopal minister,
would pause at the station to discuss with us anything
from the proper modulation of the voice to the missions
of Francis Xavier.

A great logging company made its headquarters at
the Depot for many years. It not only brought in a new
type of Negro, the guitar-playing, minstrel-like wan-
derer, but Canadians, Russians, and Chinamen. And
serving the community thus built up were several
stores of which the proprietors were good conductors of
talks. One of them, Baldy Hammill, was an expert in
local history and anecdote. The mail carrier from Vul-
tare across the river was like the ancient Nestor in rich
memories and charming narrative style. When Mamma
expressed a fear that we might be hanging around the
Depot too much, Papa remarked that he too loved to
hear Jim Jones talk. The variety of characters and the
professional skills in procession before us gave us something of the satisfaction Socrates experienced with the
artisans and philosophers of Athens.

In Uncle Charlie's law court which he held at Mr.

Iles' store, we could examine into the peccadilloes of the country-side. Sometimes questions were raised there of deep ethical and legal import. Then Papa, as Sheriff, would take the culprits to Halifax. And along the road went the whole pageant of transportation from the ox cart to the automobile. There were, close by, the ruins of Sledge's Tavern, scene of horse races and chicken fights in the old days. It was one of the haunts of Halifax County's self-appointed hero, Colonel Dan Tucker. Along this road the tobacco rollers had trundled their hogsheads on the way across the river by Old Gaston to Petersburg. And when finally the automobile came to change the ways of the country, we took pride in the fact that Arthur had brought to the county its first car.

A remarkably wide range of people patronized our shop, gin, gristmill, planing mill, and sawmill. They differed in quality from the rough, abusive, fellow who tried to start a fight in the shop to the polished gentleman who was standing by. This gentleman stopped the fight with an observation: "Consider the source and let it pass." Runaway couples, and couples not having to run away came to the house to get Uncle Charlie to marry them. He never charged a fee, but he was pressed by one happy groom to take a quarter anyway.

Company came freely. They varied in kind from Old Jones, the tramp who came periodically to fill up on food and to sleep in the office, to strangers coming up from the night train and saying: "We thought it was a hotel. But can't we stay anyway?" A delightful and frequent visitor was Mr. Joe Mason who discoursed to us on the dignity of the law and the glories of Lord Chesterfield. Always there were kinfolks company, and boys and girls just visiting. There always seemed to be room. When beds gave out we made pallets on the floor. It was my job to carry water to the girls. Many a morning I stepped over them lying on the floor and splashed water in their faces.

All of this was stimulating and disciplinary to children trying to grow up and to get at ease with folks. But I doubt if we should have been urged along the lines of social practice so constantly but for Aunt Lula. Aunt Lula had been raised in town. The countryman possesses enough virtues to concede that the townsman is, as a rule, more practiced in the amenities of dress, flowers, interior decoration, and diplomacy than the countryman. Aunt Lula gave us these aesthetic urges from our babyhood on. All of her relations lived in towns, notably Norfolk and Baltimore. They would come to visit us and bring the talk of theatres and cos-

mopolitan events to us. Aunt Lula and Uncle Charlie
would go to visit them. Sometimes they would take us
as far as Norfolk. When we got back home we would
turn the sawdust pile into the switchback like the one
we had ridden on at Ocean View. And we would put
into our school plays the histrionic fire we had thrilled
to at our first play seen in Norfolk, "Lottie the Poor
Saleslady; or Death Before Dishonor."

And when we were ripe for a fresh cultural and social urge, Aunt Winnie left us to get married. Miss
Ethel succeeded her in school. She added to the virtues
of the school, music, that most civilizing of influences.
Around her the parlor awoke to life as an instrument
of graciousness. She was truly an artist on the piano, a
disciplined student. We had tinkered at music, before
she came, under the misapprehension that about all
there was to it was ability to play by ear, or nothing.
Under her the girls all became competent piano-players.
Even Hugh and I learned to play the piano by note,
though our chief instrument remained the harmonica,
played by ear.

Miss Ethel vitalized our singing by her competence
in leading it. One day she was playing "The Holy
City" when Mr. Wake, a visitor from New York, began
to sing it. Mr. Wake's singing was a revelation in ex-

pert, trained, song. About this time, also, Joe gave us a graphophone. We played a lot of trash on it which we have forgotten. But we never tired of two records: the "Quartette" from Rigoletto, and the "Sextette" from Lucia.

Miss Ethel was trained at Oxford College under Aunt Sal and Mr. Hobgood. We never saw Mr. Hobgood at home, but Aunt Sal, Mamma's Aunt, was a constant visitor. She was a grand lady. Through her influence and Miss Ethel's, Sallie, Fannie, and Sue later went to Oxford. Miss Ethel had two delightful sisters, Lucy and Mary, who paid us a visit each year. They were Louisburg College girls, and to Louisburg, Helen and Mary were to go later. But Lucy and Mary came just at the time we younger boys were getting girl-conscious. We would work hard all day long, then dress up and giggle with them till long after midnight. Miss Ethel had a special piano piece which she played to warn the rest of us to stay out of the parlor, but to invite Henry to come in. Thus in the course of time Miss Ethel became "Sister" Ethel, and our school was closed for several years.

It was just at this time that Cousin Horace and his family came into our lives. Cousin Horace was urbane and kindly just like the Roman gentleman whose name he bore. But he differed from his Roman predecessor in one important particular. He had a large family, a delightful girl for each boy in our family, and almost enough sons to match each girl in our family with a boy. Of course we had known Cousin Horace and his family all along. But in those days of red-mud roads, the eight miles of distance which separated us were nearly impassable. It now happened that business came to the aid of society. For, as our sawmill grew, we added a railroad to it. And this railroad ran right by Cousin Horace's. We could use the train to transport our whole family to his house and to transport his whole family to our house. For minor occasions we could use the pump car.

Even though Papa and Uncle Charlie drove themselves and us through crowded days of work, they were great recognizers of holidays. On such days we took the whole neighborhood on the train to picnics on the creek—fish-frys, Brunswick stews, and Barbecues. Our two families could be counted on to put pep into any party. Our chief party was the square dance at Christmas.

Our square dances were not researches into quaint old customs. They were not chaotic and ignorant romps. They were current dances, thoroughly learned.

I used to practice the figures by the hour in the hay-loft, and I learned all the dance tunes on the harmonica. They were formal in that we danced by card schedules with a good deal of concern to see that everybody danced. There were no break dances, no wallflowers; and there was no "getting stuck."

Finances were embarrassing to us youngsters. I was very grateful to my elder brothers and cousins for quietly paying the musicians when the "men" were called together for that purpose after midnight on each dance night. I reciprocated many a time by playing all night long for the dance on my harmonica. Musicians were scarce, temperamental, and hard to engage surely.

My chief embarrassment, however, was personal. I did not have the nerve to ask the girls to dance with me. I went to several dances before I ever got up enough nerve to ask one. Finally I heard Harry ask Becky to give him the fifteenth set. I closed my eyes and rushed in.

"Will you give me the sixteenth?" I asked. She would. I regard this social venture as a victory over terror in society comparable with the victory over a similar terror at joining the Church.

Our dance master was our Sunday School teacher,

Cousin Eddie. He was a great deal more stern about manners and proficiency on the dance floor than he was over the minutiae of the catechism. I am equally grateful to him for both disciplines.

The women-folks would cook for a week to prepare the turkeys, chickens, sausages, cakes and pies for the midnight suppers. Dancing began at 8 and lasted till well into the next day. It took real food to sustain the dancers. We would help by bringing wood for all-night fires, decorating the colonnade, the parlor, and the dining room with holly, mistletoe, and running cedar. We would wax the floor, engage the solemn promise of the musicians to be there on time, and get word around near and far.

The morning train would bring a contingent from Weldon. The evening train would bring guests from Littleton and our special kin from Six-Pound. They always came in with soft-spoken gossip and delightful laughter at renewing family associations. The log train would bring in Cousin Horace and his girls and boys. Without them there simply could be no dance. There would be much eating of supper, much dressing and primping. Night would fall and all semblance of a work-a-day world would vanish. We felt that Versailles in its palmiest days could never be any more glamorous.

The floor of the colonnade would gleam in the lamp-light. Fires would crackle in the parlor, the dining room, Mamma's room, Aunt Lula's room. All these were now adjuncts to the ballroom and full of boys and girls busy arranging their schedules. Cousin Horace would urge on the bashful boys like me to perk up and ask the girls. The girls were now all mysterious and visions in white. But, after all, when one got up courage to ask them to dance, they would smile and condescend.

Sid Dunstan, brother of the famous Tom of Chapel Hill, with his banjo, a fiddler, and a mandolin player, would strike up "Light in the Window."

"Get your partners for the first set!" Cousin Eddie would call. We would scurry into lines around the four sides of the room.

"Balance all!"

The gentlemen would dance to the center of the floor, return, bow, and swing their partners.

"Forward heads!"

This command would begin a series of evolutions. The head couples would advance in a line, sway to the music, pass to opposite ends of the room, change partners, change back, promenade home and swing. The side couples would repeat the evolutions. Then would come the command:

"Swing corners, all!" Each gentleman would turn the lady on his left, then turn his partner.

Thus began the dance. After these opening movements, the dance master would call one of many figures.

"Dance to the music!" Cousin Eddie would command. The floor would rock and resound like a drum.

"First couple lead off...!" would come to start the chosen figure. Then,

"Watch that boy get about!" Cousin Eddie would shout as Hugh, the best dancer of us all, would "Chase the Squirrel."

IX.   The Principle of the Thing

"**R**OB IS OUR best tail-end man," I overheard Henry tell Papa as they were discussing who should do what at the sawmill. The tail-end man is the last man to handle lumber in the line of sawmill operations. He helps the swing-saw man cut up all the slab wood and refuse lumber, and he throws these in one pile. He receives the lumber from the big saw and the edging saw and throws it into a pile to be hauled away to the drying yards. His job is one requiring great speed and alertness rather than great strength.

I was glad to hear myself acclaimed as able to do a man's work around the sawmill. I was 15 years old. The other boys had entered on mature jobs when they were 12 years old. I had wanted to succeed in the occupation which carried prestige. The sawmill had assumed complete lead in our affairs. It had reduced the farm to an occasional sideline. The farm stock lived on bought food and appeared in Uncle Charlie's eyes to be mere pensioners on the sawmill's bounty. The shop ceased to be a general manufactory of everything from cradles to coffins, and became a repair station for sawmill machinery. The gin ran only spasmodically.

The gristmill ceased to grind corn for the farmers. It ran only to grind bought corn and oats for the stock. The stock, like us, lived not on our own home-raised food any longer. We all lived out of the grocery store, just like people in town. Uncle Johnny, the Shaws, and the Kings continued to farm. But most of the neighbors either worked at the lumber business or left their farms altogether to go to the towns and cities.

The great logging company at the Depot had speeded up lumbering. It was no longer an occupation associated with farming. It was a highly competitive business in itself. Workers in it were highly-trained specialists from the cross-cut saw men in the woods to saw filers in the mills. The old leisurely sun-time working day had disappeared. All men worked from 6 to 6 by a time clock. Even the merchants and the railroad rose and fell in business as lumber operations dictated.

All the elder boys were specialists. Henry was general

foreman, having replaced Uncle Charlie, who became general buyer and seller. Charles was mill foreman. John was locomotive engineer. Rob Bailey, a cousin in Uncle Charlie's family, was locomotive fireman. Harry was trainman. Joe had graduated from the shop to a job with Arthur in a separate mill. Ernest was feeder of the logging teams. Even Papa had ceased sheriffing for a while and had become a daily superintendent of the lumber industry.

I loved the farm and had held to this love in gradually maturing jobs in the field with cotton, corn and peanuts. But I felt the onus of low-caste work. The Negroes despised farming, which they called "private work," as much as they adored lumbering, which they called "public work." My own brothers and cousins called my work on the farm "piddling." They would go out to the railroad and the woods as to adventure in the morning. They would return at night looking sweaty but important, and jeer at me as I milked the cows.

The girls with their company aggravated my sense of inferiority by riding on the train and lavishing all their admiration on the wonderful athletic skill of the boys with canthook and chain. Nobody expressed any wonder at my skill in plowing. And one day the girls

tripped disdainfully by me to the train as I was spread-
ing manure on the garden. It made me feel keenly all
the emotions of agrarian unrest.

There was indeed color and movement in lumbering. In the woods the axe men and cross-cut saw men
would shout to the chopping of their axes and the
cling-clang of the saws. There was a sense of conquest
in felling the great trees in the warm scent of rosin,
pine straw, bruised vine and bay-flower, all slightly
flavored with kerosene from the saws. It made no difference in the triumphant feeling that fires inevitably
came along and reduced the woods to a waste of burnt
soil and tumble weed. New forests were ever at hand.
The men were athletic and alert with canthook and log
cart. The oxen and the mules, so shaggy-haired and
slow-footed on the farm, became in the log woods
lithe, quick-footed, even vicious in their speed.

The boys loaded the train as well as ran it. With
canthook and chain, and with mules who knew exactly what to do, they could swing great logs like
jackstraws. It was an athletic feat requiring the utmost
skill and concentration of mind and body, for maiming
and death awaited the incompetent. Then to the sound
of the whistle the train would move millward. Harry
would leap from car to car like a flying squirrel to

attend to the brakes. There would be a luscious pause to take on water for the locomotive at Persimmon Creek, and to eat a watermelon. No wonder the girls admired the life of these lumbermen and railroad men.

I was now at least a mill-hand. It was gruelling work. The whistle aroused us at 5:30. At 6 the engine would puff-puff-puff on the long pull and go chucka-shucka-chucka as the carriage came back. The big saw would quarrel. The edger would whine. The swing-saw would go cheep-cheep-cheep. The logs would bump on the turning blocks at one end of the mill. A steady stream of slabs, edging strips, and boards would come down on me at the other. Out would go truck loads of lumber to the drying yards, and from there dried lumber would go down to cars on the Seaboard Air Line. There were 20 minutes for breakfast at 8, 30 minutes for dinner at 12. And, unless a belt broke, there was no pause until 6 in the evening. The smell of rosin, wet sawdust, and hot water was redolent in the boiling sun. The blower would pile still higher a mountain of sawdust. And, when the mill stopped at night, steam would hiss and sputter for hours like the breath of a sleeping dragon.

I began to long for the leisure to read and dream while I grazed Old Mary or loafed at the plow. But this, like the army, was a job I couldn't lose. The 1907 panic struck the lumber business terrific blows. Hands were paid, not in cash, but in scrip. Our business survived only because there were so many boys to work without burdening the pay roll. The farm stock all went to raise cash. Old Mary refused to be part of a herd of beef cattle in the lowgrounds of Mush Island where they were pastured. She got out and ran away. I rejoice in her image as of the Scholar Gypsy, wandering in cowly reminiscence over the changing scene. For the home scene was changing.

The older children had married and grandchildren were exploring in house, field, and around the works, a new version of our childhood world. The older boys were all set in the professions of machinery and lumbering. It was time for the younger boys to grow up and with the girls to complete the school-room regime.

Miss Pattie came to run the school in its final burst of energy. She helped us all in spelling, arithmetic, and music. She gave me a pregnant suggestion: that I ought to go on to Mr. Graham in Warrenton. But I had to wait three more years for it to bear fruit.

We had worn out the old house till the nailheads stood out on little pyramids of wood on the floors. We had used up enough good old stuff to set an antique hunter wild. As the Store ceased to be necessary as a schoolroom it became a dormitory. But this did not relieve the pressure of our maturing family on the old house. Uncle Charlie now got out the fine lumber he had been storing for years and built himself a house a little way down the road. Papa never got around to repairing our house, though he put in water and electricity long before such things became current in the neighborhood. He was a long-headed, patient student of things, and never took action till he had thought through to a fundamental principle. And he loved each board and beam of the old house exactly as it was. I can recall him now, smoking on the front porch after supper, deep in contemplation of the poetry of closing day. All harsh outlines of field and woods would be plastic in the twilight, birds would twitter down to rest. Passing carts would stir up wisps of dust on the road going by in front. The evening train would roar by and shake the house. And the shout of a plow-boy would come up from the lowgrounds as in an elfin aria.

The deep sentiment of home, family, and friends was in both Papa and Uncle Charlie, for all their practicality. They were joined in it by Grandma, who, with them, had started afresh when Grandpa had died. We

never saw Grandpa. He had died when Papa and
Uncle Charlie were boys. But in the way they said
"Pa" and talked about him we could sense the genius
of Edgewood. It was a practical genius. Grandpa long
before the war had discarded slavery and had succeeded
better with hired labor. He had been a loyal Confederate, giving his sons to the war, being himself too old
to go. But he was not economically committed to the
Southern system. He took up after Appomattox where
he had laid down at Bethel. There was in him nothing
of the hall and nothing of the hut. Socially he had but
one concept: Folks are Folks. If he belonged to any
class, it was to the broadly American unwhipped class
of brains and character. I possess one souvenir of him,
a volume of Robert Burns. His motto, as exemplified
in his children, could well have been, "man's a man for
a' that."

I began to get closer to Papa and to see in him a
steady concentration on what he called "the principle
of the thing." He loved to work in the shop. He insisted
that things be in order and that tools be kept in ship-
shape fashion. He would conduct a repair job with the
professional joy of a teacher in a seminar. Uncle Charlie
would want to hurry so as to get on with the main job.
But not so Papa. He sought to master and get us to

master the principle of the thing. There was nothing he had not so mastered from a watch to a locomotive. He had a great eye for salvaging things. His favorite maxim was, "Waste not, want not." Others thought he simply loved junk. But he could reclaim what others had junked and make it useful and beautiful again.

I would ride with him on his sheriffing tours over the county. Friends would ask him a stock question: "Sheriff, would you hang me?"

"I would if I had to," Papa would reply. "All I can promise is that I would try to hang you like a gentleman."

I am glad to say that, in over 22 years as sheriff, he never had to hang anybody. He did win many friends among those he had to arrest. He never blamed a man. He simply executed the law's mandate about that man's actions. And he sought unhesitatingly in dress, in manner, in attitude, to live "like a gentleman." I laugh when I see today's moving picture caricatures of a sheriff; Papa was not that kind of a sheriff.

The girls got away to school. And my unceasing urge was to get to school, too.

"Why don't you study here?" Papa would inquire. About this time Fannie bought me Ruskin's *Sesame and Lillies*. The essay on reading fired me with a desire to read more studiously. I bought Milton and I found Shakespeare in the old books Uncle Charlie had brought home from the sale. With Webster's *Unabridged Dictionary,* Anthon's *Classical Dictionary,* and with Greek and Latin grammars, I would toil till midnight after hauling logs all day.

Papa said nothing. He got me up to work. My night hours were my own. Finally, when I was 18 years old, things economic seemed to be lightening. I brought up again my desire to go to school.

"Well, I have always wanted you to go to school," Papa responded. "It doesn't hurt a boy to learn to work and to see the principle of things."

This was all he said. I took the implied permission and made my own arrangements with Mr. Graham. Papa took me to the train for Warrenton. Just before the train arrived, he said:

"I am sending you to learn books. If you find out you don't want to do that, I have plenty for you to do here at home."

I learned books, among them Greek. Papa had no Greek. But even in so simple a thing as filing a saw he exhibited the Greek genius—art. His coordination of eye, hand, and brain was Greek artistry and practicality. When he got through with it the saw was good to look at and good to cut with. He saw into the principle of things with patient, sure, mastery, no matter what those things might be. Emerson never asked more insistently than he, "What can you do?" Both he and Uncle Charlie could do anything. They cared for us with such apparent ease that when we were little we thought they ran the world. They exhibited the spirit of Edgewood. It was a practical, humorous, thing-minded spirit, illumined by broad, matter-of-fact, human insights. It was deferential to, but critical of the more humane but less sternly competent spirit of Six-Pound. Edgewood and Six-Pound found spiritual fusion in Miss Sue, who was as practical as Edgewood. "Work's work," she could say with Governor Bell, an old Negro who helped raise Papa and Uncle Charlie. She could do any work that came along. But she knew that deeper than work, deeper than just folks unillumined there was personality, a spiritual, unceasing cultural force. No joke, no critical comment out of our practical sphere was ever aimed at the sure foundations of her queenly realm of poetry—poetry not as an escape from the world, but as the meaning of the world.

....Miss Sue would pause in her reading, mark the place in the book with her finger and look up, smiling. Her smile and her gaze always caressed us. At the same time, both were inwardly contemplating some beautiful memory elicited by what she was reading...

"Dear Cousin Ann," she might begin. We learned to pause also, and to listen. For fairyland was present again, and vibrant with humor, pathos, and affection ...Mamma was going to talk for a while of her girlhood in Six-Pound.

"Mamma, are we really descended from Sir Francis Drake?"

"We thought so. Aunt Sal even went so far as to write to Queen Victoria to inquire about the great fortune said to be waiting for the Drake heirs. And the Queen's secretary wrote her a nice letter about it all. But we never could get the fortune.

"High lineage was commonplace in Six-Pound. Everybody was descended from Sir Francis Drake, Sir Walter Raleigh, and Sir John Hawkins. We preferred not to inquire too closely. It was a tradition handed down to us by older people whom we loved and never doubted. And they felt the same way about the still older people who handed it down to them.

"We were at least descended from those Drakes, Raleighs, and Hawkinses who were the ancestors of Sir Francis, Sir Walter, and Sir John. We loved and admired each other so much that we merely accepted these great ones as partners and kinsmen. We thought we too conferred lustre on the names.

"We laughed about the fortune and dreamed in our poverty after the War of what it would mean to us. When we lived at Shocco Springs with Uncle John, and he would come home late at night after we had gone to bed, and knock on the front door, Cousin Ann and I would grab each other and giggle:

"There's Sir Francis, bringing us our fortune!'

"Alas, we knew nothing of fortune! All was gone in the War. Grandpa could never realize what had happened. He went to Warrenton and they were raising money for the Methodist Church there. Grandpa subscribed fifty dollars when he had just lost his whole plantation. But he worked and paid it.

"The plantation which Grandpa had lost was one which Great Grandpa had given to his daughter Winnifred when she was married. Great Grandpa had eleven girls. Each one married in the neighborhood, and each one received a plantation as a dower. Thence sprang a neighborhood of every variety of relationship, mostly expressed by the word 'Cousin.' Young Cousin Nathan even called the Negroes 'Cousin,' so habitual was the kindred-loving form of greeting."

"Mamma, tell us about where you lived."

"Well, we did not have large houses. Mr. Plumtree built a house which we thought very grand. It had just three rooms, one on top of the other, with stairsteps leading up from the corner of the rooms. Just before the War, Old Cousin Nathan built 'Millbrook.' I have seen fifty Negro mammies on Sundays with babies whose mothers and fathers were upstairs for dinner. Cousin Nathan said he wanted to die when he could no longer have the whole of Hebron congregation to dinner on Sunday.

"And there was the 'High House' down toward the river. That was a large house, where Cousin Alice lived. Cousin Billy would come there to court her. He would sit on his horse under the balcony, and Cousin Alice would come out and lean on the railing to talk to him. We could see them there almost every night.

"But your Grandpa's house was old and small, like the end of a long hall cut off and plumped down among the elms. And my Grandpa's house, where we first lived, was small, but very graceful in a grove and garden. Around it were the carriage house, the smoke-house, the kitchen, and houses for the Negroes, with a great pasture leading down through the fields to the creek. The graveyard joined right on to the front yard, and we played in this. It seemed home-like and intimate to us. We felt that our loved ones lying there played with us too. It was not a place to fear, but a presence to enjoy."

"Did you have slaves, Mamma?"

"Yes, we had a few field-hands, and their masters worked in the fields with them. In the house there were Mammy and the cook, and Caesar, the carriage-driver. When company would come, Caesar would put on a white coat and wait on the table. Aunt Sal had Dillie to wait on her. She was a child, and she played with us. One day we poured all of Aunt Sal's medicines into the top drawer of her medicine chest and stirred them together. Aunt Sal caught us and gave us all a switching.

"The Negroes and we seldom thought about slavery. We grew up together and thought of each other as belonging together in one family and on one place. But it was not always beautiful.

"Grandpa endorsed a note for a friend who couldn't pay it, and Grandpa couldn't pay it either, without selling some of the Negroes. And I can still hear Mammy weeping:

"Miss Sallie, dey done sold my onliest gal.'

"We thought slavery was right because we grew up with it. We did not know what else to do with the Negroes. And the war was brewing. The men would get mad when they talked politics. It was a crime to own a copy of Hinton Rowan Helper's book. The great book, our men-folks thought, was by Doctor Smith of Randolph-Macon College, on 'The Philosophy and Practice of Slavery.' This was printed and distributed in large quantities. It tried to teach that slavery was ordained by God. But, against all Doctor Smith and the men-folks could say, I have always heard Mammy's lament. We were blind, and we were led by the blind."

"Tell us about the war, Mamma."

"I can't. You must read Mary Johnston and Thomas

Nelson Page. 'Marse Chan' and 'Meh Lady' are the truest pictures ever drawn of what we felt, fought for, and suffered over.

"The men would ride away, and most of them never came back. Uncle John Eldridge came home on a furlough to marry Aunt Sal. He went back and was killed in the next battle, Spotsylvania, I think. He had Aunt Sal's picture over his heart. A lady there saw it, corresponded with Aunt Sal, and helped her to get his body home after the war.

"Aunt Sal, always in black, always straight as an arrow, always teaching young people and taking up for them! She never, in all her long life with us, opened her mouth about the war. She carried its banner in the silent recesses of her spirit.

"Sometimes the men would come home sick and wounded to be nursed. Cousin Horace sat for months in the parlor at Millbrook with his leg strapped to a ring in the ceiling. It was from that your Cousin Malvern got his name, Malvern Hill.

"The women and children worked and waited and prayed over news that never was clear, and always more and more terrible.

"There were refugees. One was Mr. Finley, a Northern merchant fleeing from Eastern Carolina. He supported himself by a little store he set up in a room at Millbrook. The Finleys married into the family and their descendants are your cousins.

"We had no money, and there was little to buy whenever we got some. I remember seeing Santa Claus. He was filling my stocking with peanuts. I ran away, and next morning I found he had also brought me a doll. Its body was a corncob, the shuck was the dress, and the head was a hickory nut.

"The Yankees came and camped in the grove, and we ran, too, as refugees to Warrenton.

"I was swinging on the gate when the Yankees marched through Warrenton. One of them laughed when he saw me, grabbed me, and hugged me.

" 'Here's my girl!' he said.

"The men came home and tried to work, but the war had made them forget how. They were restless and demoralized. They did not know how to have any fun. They thought they could find some in drinking.

"But they were innocently funny and gentlemanly about it.

"Three, whom we will call Cousin Cas, Cousin Bob, and Cousin Ben, had a system to keep from bothering the ladies. One would send word to the other two that it was his time to get drunk. The other two would come and take care of him in his room. They would not drink with him, but would stay sober themselves and keep him away from the ladies until his spree was over. Then they would go home, and each would take his turn at getting drunk with two sober friends to care for him.

"The women never let on that they knew what their men were doing. The women were the responsible members of the family. They ran things and kept the men from complete demoralization.

"Cousin Ann was married now and had a house full of children. She never had any money. But she knew how to make pretty things out of rags. She nearly sewed her eyes out. But all her children grew up knowing how to dress beautifully and to be gay.

"Papa taught school. He never knew how to work with his hands. He used to come down here and see the farm, the shop, and the sawmill. He never could understand how people could find so much to do, or find how to do it.

"He was jolly and gentle, and always loved home. When he was a boy he went to Randolph-Macon College. But he came home and never would go back. He said he would rather have a seat on the tongue of the ox-cart at home than in the President's chair.

"The boys at school would play jokes on him, and he would pretend to whip them and make a big noise. But he did not have the heart to whip anybody.

"He loved to go over to Millbrook and argue with Cousin Horace on 'Populism' and 'the money question.' Cousin Horace had a practical mind and could puncture Papa's arguments. Papa would get mad and come home, vowing that he was 'done with Horace.' But next day he would go back.

"Cousin Horace was a scholar and a successful farmer. He saved his place and even improved it. He was lame and had to run things by shouting from the porch.

"'Poor barbarian! Poor barbarian!' he would moan in exasperation at Negroes and whites who could not, or would not, understand what he wanted done.

"Cousin Horace's was a great gathering-place for all the young folks and a home for many dependents. There was Cousin Clay, who walked in his sleep, right out of an upstairs window, and landed on his head in the rockgarden. There was Uncle Kit who loved to spell out the chapters of the Bible. He would carefully mark the place of his last reading. The boys would move his marker back and he would never know the difference. He would still hope some day to have read the whole Bible.

" 'Bud' lived in Cousin Horace's yard. 'Bud' never did anything but feed the hounds. And when they had to break up the pack, he retired to the fireside and sat in a chair for three years without ever undressing or going to bed. He never would take off his hat, and his hair grew through it."

Mamma would hesitate.

"We loved each other so much, stood so much together, and got so much fun out of our troubles. It was all homey and folksy."

A young settler, exploring a new grant in this wilderness, was crossing the creek and musing over what should be the names of things. Accidentally he dropped six pounds of precious sugar into the water. He knew how to laugh at himself.

"Six-Pound Creek," he chuckled, "and this is Six-Pound Township."

A name born in a chuckle carried the spirit of laughter ever after—not bitter or harsh laughter at others, but gentle, thoughtful, self-analyzing laughter at one's self, one's folks, one circumstances.

It was a spirit none-the-less laborious for being gay. For it turned the wilderness into a garden and adorned it with gentle beauty, fragrant roses, and rollicking song—black folks and white folks in amity.

It was all the more a religious spirit for being always joyous and rejuvenant—building Hebron as part of the family scene. Hebron embraced literary and philosophical minds responsive to the devotion of the great Bishop Asbury, himself. But it embraced, also, the soul of black Aunt Becky. She would shout on the rock pile and whirl away in ecstasy down the path to the spring. And one day she returned from some seventh heaven rejoicing that it had been given her to minister to the Lord Jesus. She had made him a pair of pants, she said, and they fitted him better than any he ever had.

It was a gallant spirit, knowing how to walk the minuet and whisper sweet nothings in garden, or porch, and in parlor—when there was peace. In war it walked unflinchingly through all but the fires of hell. And it could make jokes at disaster, even as it went out to meet it.

I, too, have been in Arcadia, for I have lived in modern Six-Pound. But all I saw there was but "a symbol of a thing signified."

I have fished and waded in Six-Pound Creek. It meanders sourly today through bogs and alder thickets. But I saw it through Mamma's eyes, running trim and smooth through field and pasture where there were "cattle on a thousand hills." I heard again through Mamma's ears the protest of a Six-Pound troubador comparing his love to the creek's pools and races. "Think not my love, now quiescent, is fickle. It pauses like yon stream for a moment and gathers strength to renew its flow."

I have climbed Hebron Hill and worshipped in the little chapel. That alone is as it might have been, except there was no rumble of arriving carriages, no swish of crinoline, as ladies bounded to the ground. I have slept under the oaks at Millbrook and have heard the pack in full cry. And there seemed to ride with them a host of ghostly hunters.

For Progress has foreclosed its mortgage on all of Six-Pound except the memory and the dream. "Progress toward what?" the quizzical humor of Six-Pound might well ask. For beauty, love, and joy are not goals of Progress. They are ever-present and imperishable qualities of the spirit.